Coming Home to Myself

~

A Memoir

by Pamela Harman Daugavietis

Chapbook Press

Schuler Books
2660 28th Street SE
Grand Rapids, MI 49512
(616) 942-7330
www.schulerbooks.com

Coming Home to Myself: A Memoir
by Pamela Harman Daugavietis

ISBN 13: 9781943359103

Library of Congress Control Number: 2015948696

Copyright © 2015 Pamela Harman Daugavietis

All rights reserved.
No part of this book may be reproduced or utilized in any form or by any means electronic or mechanical, including photocopying, recording, or by any information storage and retrieval system without permission in writing from the publisher.

Published by Pamela H. Daugavietis: pamdaugavietis@icloud.com
Printed in the United States of America by Chapbook Press

Profits from the sale of this book support

Helen DeVos Children's Hospital Child Life Program;

Habitat for Humanity for Kent County; and

Girls Incorporated® at the Y.W.C.A. of West Michigan

Cover photo: The author at age three.

The Road Not Taken

by Robert Frost

Two roads diverged in the yellow woods,
And sorry I could not travel both
And be one traveler, long I stood
And looked down one as far as I could
To where it bent in the undergrowth;

Then took the other, 'twas just as fair,
And having perhaps the better claim,
Because it was grassy and wanted wear;
Though as for that the passing there
Had worn them really about the same,

And both that morning equally lay
In leaves no step had trodden black.
Oh, I kept the first for another day!
Yet knowing how way leads on to way,
I doubted if I should ever come back.

I shall be telling this with a sigh
Somewhere ages and ages hence:
Two roads diverged in a wood, and I—
I took the one less traveled by,
And that has made all the difference.

A person travels the world in search of what s/he needs
and returns home to find it.

George Moore
Irish Novelist (1852 - 1933)

Home is both the beginning and the end.
Home is not a sentimental concept at all,
but an inner compass and a North Star at the same time.
It is a metaphor for the soul.

Richard Rohr, OFM
Founder of the Center of Action and
Contemplation in Albuquerque, NM.
(1943 -   )

Dedication

To our children, parents and siblings whose love and support made our life-changing, mid-life adventure in Saudi Arabia possible.

And to our 12 grandchildren with a bit of advice, first given to a young Native American at the time of her/his initiation:

As you go the way of life, you will see a great chasm.
Jump.
It is not as wide as you think.[1]

With much love to all,
Mom/Pam/Grandma Pam

---

1 From *A Joseph Campbell Companion: Reflections on the Art of Living,* Selected and Edited by Diane K. Osbon

Author's Note

Anyone who has written and self-published a memoir knows it takes encouragement, inspiration and hands-on assistance from many others to complete. Heartfelt gratitude goes to family members and friends who provided important feedback after reading my first draft. Words cannot express my appreciation for your time, talent and honest critique. I hope you all can see your invaluable suggestions reflected in this final publication. I hesitate to name names at risk of leaving someone out. If I have, please forgive me. You, too, had an essential role in helping my dream come true.

That said, some of the following individuals read my first draft in its entirety and encouraged me to share it with a larger audience. Others took extra time to provide invaluable suggestions for rewrites and editing. To all of you I am eternally grateful: Amina Abu-Bakare, Katie and Sean Cuddihy, Georgia and Gholi Darehshori, Andy, Ray and George Daugavietis, John Harman Dickey, Julie Judd, Sally Martin, Carol Masselink and Bart Brandmiller, Deb Moore, Jan and Frank Parkinson, Jacqueline Schaefer, Lyn and Frank Spies, and Pauline and Zigfrids Zadvinskis.

Finally, I wish to thank Andy for his love and encouragement the past 26 years; without him by my side, I never would have taken "the road less traveled" . . . *and that has made all the difference.*

Table of Contents

Introduction		Page 8
Chapter 1	*Off to the Desert*	Page 13
Chapter 2	*Settling In*	Page 23
Chapter 3	*A Dream Come True*	Page 36
Chapter 4	*The 'Magic' Kingdom*	Page 45
Chapter 5	*Honeymoon in Turkey*	Page 56
Chapter 6	*New Opportunity*	Page 79
Chapter 7	*Cultural Differences*	Page 89
Chapter 8	*Princesses' School*	Page 96
Chapter 9	*Christmas in Riyadh*	Page 114
Chapter 10	*Prince Abdullah's Visit*	Page 123
Chapter 11	*King Faisal Foundation*	Page 130
Chapter 12	*Ramadan*	Page 140
Chapter 13	*Marianne Alireza*	Page 146
Chapter 14	*Emmanuel*	Page 156
Chapter 15	*The Invasion*	Page 164
Chapter 16	*A Daring Adventure*	Page 177
Chapter 17	*Ahmet's Wedding*	Page 185
Chapter 18	*Impending War*	Page 196
Chapter 19	*Masalama*	Page 213
Chapter 20	*Going Home*	Page 225
Epilogue		Page 231
References		Page 235

Introduction

We live our lives forward but we understand them backward.
—Kierkegaard

The year I turned 37, I found myself at a formidable crossroads. For inspiration, I taped a copy of Robert Frost's familiar poem, *The Road Not Taken*, to my refrigerator. I read it over and over again as I pondered its sobering message. Once I started down one road, I knew I would never come back to where I had begun. My 14-year marriage was about to end, and with two young sons to raise, ages 11 and 8, my future looked bleak.

A poetry lover all my life, I memorized Frost's classic as a constant reminder that I, too, would find the wisdom when the time came to choose the best road to travel. I didn't want my sons to feel responsible for the breakup of their parents' marriage because they weren't. During the early months of 1980 when such thoughts dominated my waking hours, I never imagined how far away I would eventually travel to discover the true meaning of 'home.'

Up to this point, I had enjoyed a near-idyllic upbringing in the American Midwest, in a white, Christian, middle-class family. I believed in God and felt I was living as my parents, my religion, and my culture taught me to live. Still, in my late 30s, I was beginning to feel adrift. I faced challenges I wasn't prepared to face, and I didn't know why.

My life went on, of course, and Frost's poem went with me as I moved from one address to another and a new job in a city away from my sons. I had to trust that I was making the right decisions for the right reasons, for them and for me. I couldn't envision how my future, or theirs, would unfold, but I knew I wanted someday to marry a man who shared my values and dreams for a real home together with our families.

When Andy Daugavietis proposed marriage on September 11, 1988, it seemed my dream was beginning to come true. We had dated for five years, even though I now lived and worked in Grand Rapids, Michigan. He still practiced medicine at Burns Clinic in Petoskey and his son Peter would soon graduate from Petoskey High School. His daughter Leis lived in Tallahassee, Florida with her mother and was a junior at Leon High School. My sons John and Bob lived with their dad and Bridget, their stepmother, in Petoskey. John was a freshman at Hillsdale College and Bob was a junior at Petoskey High School.

What I had not expected was Andy calling two weeks later to tell me he had a job offer in Riyadh, Saudi Arabia. I knew he had received an offer six months earlier from King Faisal Hospital in Riyadh, but he couldn't get his affairs in order in time to accept the position. I was mistaken when I assumed that would be the end of his desire for a mid-life adventure in the Middle East.

"The mail just came," he said excitedly. "King Fahad National Guard Hospital is offering me a two-year contract as a senior staff consultant in rheumatology. If I accept, I have to report to work on January 10th."

"Andy, that's only four months from today."

"Yes, isn't it great? Should we accept?"

I took a deep breath, then heard myself say, "Yes, let's go."

I couldn't wait to telephone my mother in Worthington, Ohio. When I told her we were engaged, she was thrilled. I had no details to share except that Andy had to report to the hospital in Riyadh by January 10th. I would move back to Petoskey to look after Peter, pack up Andy's belongings, sell his house and prepare to leave for Saudi Arabia after Peter's graduation and our wedding.

I knew I would someday write the book you hold in your hands, mostly for our children. I wanted them to understand how our mid-life adventure started and why we took "the road less traveled" by going to Saudi Arabia 26 years ago. I wanted them to know that whatever hardships any of us experienced because of the decisions Andy and I made have actually strengthened us. We learned to better appreciate our faith, family, friends and community and the freedoms we enjoy as Americans. I wanted them to know we did what we did out of love for them, and for our own happiness and wellbeing as well as theirs.

Writing my memoir has given me more angst and has been more time consuming than I imagined. Now that it's completed, I realize the process of writing about the facts of our adventure and my associated emotions and feelings about them—both then and now—has benefitted me more than anyone.

As Mark Matousek, an American memoirist, writing coach and journalist says, "When you tell the truth your story changes, and when your story changes your life changes."

After my divorce, the story I told myself was that my life was over. Everything I valued, everything I worked hard to achieve, everything I thought had defined me— my marriage, my home, and being a mother to my two sons—had been lost. When I looked in a mirror, I saw a victim and an unappreciated martyr. At the time, I didn't realize how naïve and inexperienced I was. Instead, I was too trusting, too eager to please others by giving myself away.

The truth was that marrying Andy and going with him to Saudi Arabia was the most difficult decision I ever made; yet, it was the best decision I ever made. I came to understand the power of paradox to change my dualistic 'either/or' thinking to non-dual 'both/and' thinking. Meeting people from around the world taught me the value of diversity. I learned to accept other cultures, religions, ethnicities and traditions as interesting rather than reasons to be fearful of those different from me. I learned that first impressions aren't always accurate. I learned that real heroes are those who reach across false boundaries that divide us as humans to show selfless courage in times of crisis and uncertainty. I also learned I had more courage, more confidence, more compassion for others and myself than I ever realized.

I learned my story is not all about me. My story is shared with girls and women around the world who are taught to believe they are 'less than' men. My story is also THE story of humanity—the story that all of us are created and sustained by the same loving and omnipotent God that created the Universe. We breathe the same air; we drink the same water. We all depend on the same Sun to warm our planet and grow our food. We all need the love of family and friends to live lives of meaning and purpose. I truly believe that we have the ability, if we can muster the collective will, to someday write the story of how we, as inhabitants of the same planet, came together as One, during this critical time in history, to create a world that works for everyone.

Even though at the time some experiences were painful, I now see everything that happened more than 25 years ago from a positive perspective. I can look back on what occurred before, during and after our time in Saudi Arabia with forgiveness and humor. I rediscovered my love of writing, especially real stories about real people who make a positive difference in the lives of others. I learned to 'lighten up' and quit taking myself so seriously. I learned that every human life born into our world has intrinsic potential and divine power for good. I learned that thoughts lead us to choices that create our reality, personally and collectively, by what we choose to think and how we choose to live.

Lastly, I have learned that writing one's memoir can be the most rewarding and healing experience for anyone with a desire to do so. If you feel inspired to write your own memoir, I hope you will find the resources listed in the back of this book as helpful to you as they have been to me.

Chapter 1

Off to the Desert

With just minutes to spare, we made it to our gate in Terminal 1 at JFK International. Travelers arriving and departing from all over the world filled the concourse. Never in my life had I seen such a vast diversity of faces—men, women and children of different color and ethnicity—all dressed in strange apparel and chattering away in strange languages. When I told Andy I wanted to call the boys and Mother one last time before boarding, he winced.

"Make it brief," he said, glancing at his watch.

Lucky to find a pay phone close by, I slid a fistful of quarters into the coin slot. When no one answered in Petoskey, I hung up, slid the quarters back into the phone and dialed Mother's number in Worthington. She answered on the first ring.

"Hello," she said, in her usual cheery voice.

"Mommy! It's me. We made it to New York!"

"What time does your flight leave?"

"Not until nine. We board in a few minutes."

The lump in my throat was so huge I could hardly swallow. Mother had been my Rock of Gibraltar all my life, the person I could count on as my pillar of strength. Saying goodbye to her when I moved from Worthington to Petoskey 20 years earlier was painful but saying good-bye to her now was more difficult.

Overhead, a loud, resonant female voice announced flights departing to exotic cities around the world— London, Paris, Cairo, Istanbul, Hong Kong, Johannesburg, and Riyadh. The only country I had ever visited outside of the U.S.A. was Canada. My chest tightened as I thought about actually being on the plane leaving for Riyadh, Saudi Arabia, so far from home.

"Mother, I have to hang up now. Please tell the boys we made it to New York. I'll call as soon as I can after we arrive in Riyadh. Don't know when, but I will call."

I hung up the receiver and paused to wipe tears from my face. I didn't want Andy and Leis to know I was homesick already. Leis was Bob's age—going into her senior year of high school. She would spend six weeks with us before returning to Florida. I wished John and Bob could have come, too, but visas were issued only to employed expatriates and their dependents. John and Bob weren't our dependents, and they had summer jobs.

Once Andy, Leis and I had settled into our economy-class seats aboard a double-decker Saudia Airlines 747, female flight attendants demonstrated safety instructions. I had never flown on such a large plane— three seats on both sides of the cabin separated by six interior seats. Andy was by the window; I was in the middle, and Leis was on the aisle.

Overhead lights in the passenger area dimmed. The roar of the engines grew louder and louder. A male voice joined the din shouting indistinguishable words from overhead. Andy noticed my startled look.

"Muslim prayers, in Arabic, for a safe flight," he said.

We pulled away from the gate and taxied onto the runway, picking up speed. Everything inside the passenger area rattled and shook as we lumbered along. I couldn't believe something so massive could lift off the ground. I had never flown across an ocean before, so knowing we'd be cruising at 35,000 feet with no place to land in case of an emergency gave me pause.

As our plane continued to climb, an image of a huge eagle taking flight came to mind. I thought of the Bible verse read at my father's funeral two years earlier, Isaiah 40:31. *They that wait upon the Lord shall renew their strength; they shall mount up with wings as eagles; they shall run, and not be weary, and they shall walk, and not faint.*

Daddy loved eagles. He was a staunch Republican, a lifelong Methodist and an active leader in our church. What would he think of me, his middle daughter, going off to Saudi Arabia with her new husband? Would he approve of me becoming Catholic so Andy and I could be married at St. Francis Church in Petoskey three days ago?

The Arabic prayer continued as we lifted higher and higher into the sky. I didn't understand what this fellow was saying, but I knew he was praying to the same God I was praying to in English. I trusted all our prayers for a safe flight, regardless of language or religious tradition, would be heard and answered. I closed my eyes and drifted off to sleep only to be awakened soon afterward by loud ripping sounds and a forceful bump against the back of my seat. I sat up and grabbed Andy's arm.

"What was that?" I said as another bump rocked my seat, and then another. We could hear cloth tearing, not just once but repeated tearing and ripping sounds.

"What is going on back there?" I whispered to Leis. This time I raised myself up enough to peer over the top of my seat. The lights in the cabin were dim, yet I could see passengers behind us ripping up what looked like sheets. They were undressing and wrapping themselves in long, white swathes of cloth while bumping up against the backs of our seats.

I needed to go to the toilet, so I figured I'd get a better and longer look when I returned to my seat. When I opened the lavatory door, I was met with another surprise—a rainforest! Water dripped from the ceiling and ran down the walls, the mirror, and onto the sink and floor of the tiny space. Good grief, I wondered. What's going on here? I wiped off the toilet seat and with some difficulty managed to maneuver myself around the soggy enclosure without getting my long skirt wet.

By the time I returned to my seat, the passengers behind us were sitting quietly, wrapped in loosely fitting white cloth. I whispered to Andy and Leis that I had encountered another surprise.

"You won't believe the lavatory. There's water everywhere."

"Muslims wash before they pray," Andy said, without looking up from the book he was reading. "They're all going to the Hajj, in Mecca."

"Oh," I said, as I marveled at all these cultural and religious differences I was discovering even before we arrived in the desert.

"What's the hajj?" I finally asked, more curious about where we would soon be living than embarrassed about my ignorance.

"It's one of the five pillars of Islam, an annual pilgrimage all able-bodied Muslims are required to take at least once in a lifetime. It's supposedly the largest worldwide gathering of Muslims every year."

"So why do they dress in torn sheets?"

"Something about showing equality regardless of wealth or status. Men wear seamless white cloth; women cover their hair and wear loose clothing."

Later in the flight, after dinner, I awoke from another interruption. A flight attendant hurried down the aisle, glancing right and left at sleeping passengers.

"Doctor? Is there a doctor here? Doctor, please?" she said.

Andy, too, had fallen asleep, but Leis and I were reading. I grabbed his arm and held it high in the air so the flight attendant could see him. He gave me a surprised look, but before he could pull his arm down, the flight attendant stopped and spoke directly to him.

"Sir, can you come with me, please?

Leis and I looked at each other with wide eyes, trying to imagine who was sick and wondering if Andy would be able to help. Soon, he returned and began digging through my carry-on. Once he found what he was looking for, he told us he'd be right back. When he returned, he said a young Saudi woman traveling in first class had an acute bladder infection.

"I gave her several of your antibiotic capsules to last until she gets home," he said.

"Who is she?" I asked.

"Didn't ask. Don't know."

Within minutes, the flight attendant reappeared, smiling warmly.

"Because of your kindness, Doctor," she said, speaking directly to Andy, "the family, who prefers to remain anonymous, wishes to offer you and your family seating in business class."

We quickly gathered our belongings and followed the attendant up a flight of stairs. We entered a spacious area furnished with thick carpeting and leather seating with large oblong-shaped windows along both sides.

Two male flight attendants greeted us, took our carry-ons and showed us to our large, reclining leather seats with generous legroom. We settled into our new surroundings with feelings of gratitude toward our mysterious benefactor. The homesickness I'd felt since we left NYC was still there, but it wasn't my only emotion. I was also feeling excited and happily impressed by our good fortune.

Now at cruising altitude and halfway through our 13-hour flight, the seatbelt sign was off to we could get up and walk into the lounge area to peer out the windows. With no clouds in the sky, the scene below was astounding. We were flying directly over a part of the world I had only seen in textbooks. We could easily identify the Mediterranean Sea and the Nile River snaking through Egypt. As tired as I was, I felt stirrings of curiosity and even a bit of courage welling up inside. Maybe I would enjoy this adventure after all, in spite of missing my boys and feeling insecure as an inexperienced traveler.

As we began our descent, I could see in the distance a shimmering carpet of pulsating lights floating on an endless expanse of black nothingness. From 10,000 feet in the air, Riyadh cast an enormous, radiant glow high into the night sky. As our plane neared the ground, tiny dots of flickering light twinkled on and off across the flat desert surrounding the city.

"What are those little dots of light?" I asked.

"Bedouin campfires," Andy said. "Bedouins are desert people—goat, sheep and camel herders. They're part of the Saudi Arabian National Guard, protectors of the Kingdom's oil fields, my patients I see every day in the clinic."

While not as huge as JFK, the King Khalid International Airport was larger than I imagined, a modern, marble and glass structure with lofty ceilings, skylights, and atriums. At this late hour, the airport at first appeared to be deserted. Our planeload of tired passengers walked in silence down the narrow stairway toward the main floor and then to immigration, an enormous open space with high ceilings. We were surprised to see hundreds of people lined up in two lines along the left side of the arena—one for females, one for males. Most of them wore white shirts or light blue uniforms.

"They're the workers," Andy said, "the gardeners, maids, maintenance and construction workers— mostly Filipinos, Bangladeshis, Yemenis, and African."

We took our place in the line for expatriate business and medical professionals and American Embassy staff. Those with Saudi passports stood in a middle line that moved more quickly than the other two lines. After a 20-minute wait, we handed our passports to an expressionless male Saudi official. He looked us and our passports over, asked where we were from, why we were there and for how long. He stamped them and handed them back to us without comment.

Next, we were directed to collect our suitcases and move through customs. If customs officials found anything unlawful, they would confiscate whatever offended them and possibly detain us. As tired as I was physically, I became wide-awake mentally. Would customs officials find and confiscate my Bible? A friend of a friend who had lived in Saudi Arabia said to wrap it in sanitary napkins to prevent male customs agents from touching it. I prayed whoever searched my suitcase would be tired and see us off and on our way as quickly as possible.

After waiting half an hour, we finally reached a conveyor belt that whisked our bags to a table where a uniformed male Saudi official opened and searched through them one at a time. Andy and Leis each had one large suitcase, and I had two huge suitcases and another smaller one. The agent opened the one with my Bible in it and moved his hands swiftly among clothing, books, assorted shoes, and toiletries. Thankfully, he avoided the corner where I had stashed my more personal items. I stared straight ahead while silently praying over and over, *please protect my Bible, please protect my Bible.* He opened several books and leafed through the pages. He checked labels on some of the bottles of lotion and shampoo wrapped in plastic bags. Finally, he said, "Halas[2]," and motioned for me to close my suitcase and take it away.

    One by one, we loaded our bags onto a large trolley. With Andy in the lead pushing the trolley, we headed for the lobby filled with people, few Westerners among them, waiting for arriving passengers. A tall, dark-skinned man wearing a turban appeared out of the crowd calling to Andy.

    "Doctor, doctor," he said, waving his hands, his gold teeth lighting up his already warm and welcoming smile.

    "Mohammed, meet my wife and daughter," Andy said, reaching out to shake his hand. Fortunately, I did not have a hand to offer Mohammed, who did not offer his hand to me. I had momentarily forgotten that Muslim males do not shake hands with females. Instead, Mohammed bowed to us respectfully and reached for my carry-on. I gladly handed it over.

    "The car is waiting," he said to Andy, motioning for all of us to follow him through the automatic revolving doors to the curb where his six-seat Ranger was parked.

    After we left the entranceway to the airport, the Ranger's headlights led us through the darkness until we were out on the four-lane highway. Occasionally, we'd see a Bedouin campfire flickering in the desert that looked like little dots of light from the sky. Soon, on the left, we could see along the road the high fence enclosure surrounding the King Fahad National Guard Hospital compound. Mohammed slowed as we approached the lighted

---

[2] It's finished.

security entrance where we were met by armed guards standing on either side of the van. After Andy handed over our passports and showed them his official hospital badge, they waved us in. Five minutes later, we were pulling into the driveway of our new home, a two-story, three-bedroom villa at 153 Al Awzae Street, also surrounded by its own private wall.

"Welcome home," Andy said as he unlocked the side door into the utility room. "Wait here."

He set down his briefcase and reached inside to turn on overhead lights. He walked through the kitchen and disappeared around the corner. Soon, we could hear his footsteps echoing on the floors in the other rooms. Exhausted at such a late hour after traveling for more than 24 hours, I staggered through the nondescript but spacious kitchen, squinting my eyes against glaring ceiling lights. In contrast, the walls and high ceilings were painted a drab tan color. The brightly lit hallway revealed more tan walls and high ceilings, more white marble floors. My proud husband was waiting there for Leis and me, pointing to side-by-side living rooms.

"One for male guests, one for female guests," he said, smiling.

I peered into the identical rooms, each with a few pieces of dark brown upholstered furniture, dark brown tribal rugs on the floor, and a large, window air conditioner. From there, Andy led us into the dining room with seating for ten around a large, heavy wooden table. Again, all four walls were tan and bare. A guest lavatory off the dining room had a Saudi-style toilet meaning the toilet was a hole in the floor, requiring the user to squat rather than sit. The other guest lavatory off the main hallway was a Western-style, sit-upon toilet. Both lavatories were spotlessly clean and completely tiled in white porcelain with marble floors.

From the main hallway, a marble staircase led to a sizeable family room on the second floor, sparsely furnished like the rooms downstairs. The master bedroom was off to the right, with a king-size bed, end tables and lamps, two large, wooden armoires, and a private bath with a bathtub, shower, and a Western-style toilet. Two additional bedrooms off to the left shared a full bath with a Western-style toilet.

Andy pointed to the marble stairway from the first to the second floor that continued up to a single third-floor doorway that opened onto a terrace.

"The view up there is stunning," he said. "On a clear day, you have a 360-degree, birds-eye view of our compound and the surrounding desert."

"I'll check it out tomorrow," I said. "I'm exhausted."

We hauled our luggage upstairs and unpacked enough essentials to clean up and go to bed. I wondered how long it would take to feel comfortable in a villa that looked more like a mausoleum than a home. Too tired to talk, I kept my thoughts to myself. Andy seemed so proud of our villa. I didn't want him to know I wasn't as impressed as he seemed to be with our first home together. Perhaps I'd feel better in the morning.

Within an hour of falling into a deep sleep, I awoke when a loud, male voice, began wailing, "Allah Akbar; Allah Akbar[3]."

"What in the world is that?" I asked my sleeping husband.

"The muezzin[4]'s calling the faithful to prayer," he mumbled. "The mosque is behind us in the next block. You'll get used to it."

Andy rolled over and pulled the covers over his head while I lay there wondering what other surprises were in store for me.

---

[3] God is greater.
[4] A man who calls Muslims to prayer from the minaret of a mosque.

Chapter 2

Settling In

Andy turned off the window air conditioner and pulled open the drapes. Bright sunlight streamed into our bedroom as I slowly opened my eyes. I had been sleeping on and off since we arrived, trying to adjust to local time.

"Time to get up," he said. "Orientation begins at 7:30. We have an hour to get to the bus stop. Breakfast is ready downstairs."

I climbed out of bed and paused to look out the large bedroom window facing east. The morning sun cast a golden, monochromatic glow over the entire neighborhood. Villas identical to ours, each surrounded by its own high, sand-colored wall, lined both sides of Al Awzae Street with no trees, grass, or landscaping in sight. Looking straight ahead, only the top of the mosque's prayer tower was visible over the roofs of the villas.

"Leis is up, " Andy hollered from the hallway.

"Okay, thanks," I said. "I'll take a quick shower and come down for breakfast."

Refreshed after my first shower in three days, and a tasty breakfast of coffee, orange juice and buttered toast with strawberry jam, I started to feel stirrings of curiosity about our new neighborhood and the compound that was now our home.

"We have to leave in a few minutes," said Andy. "Make sure you have everything you need before we go. Don't forget sunglasses."

He also cautioned Leis and me never to leave the villa without bottled water, a necessity when walking outside, especially in the summer.

He kept a supply of filled water bottles in the freezer for convenience. They defrosted quickly and stayed colder longer.

"The bus stops several blocks behind our villa," he said. "Let's go. We don't want to miss it."

Andy liked showing and telling us all the rules and regulations of compound life. He wanted us to be as independent as possible after he went back to work. Walking through the outside door of our courtyard, he led us to the right and then straight-ahead through the walkway between our villa and the one next door. The sun beat down with intense, dry heat, even at this early hour. Within the compound, the neighborhood appeared deserted except for several females wearing black abayas, waiting by the bus stop at the far end of the street.

The abaya is a shapeless, black, shroud-like garment all Saudi or expat females past puberty are required to wear in public. Called burka or chador in other Muslim countries, the Saudi abaya is an essential first purchase for all expat females. Since abayas were required and we didn't have ours yet, I was worried about being stopped by a mutawa[5]. I had heard frightening stories about how they hassled females, Muslim and non-Muslim alike, for perceived offenses. One of them was not being properly covered in public.

"You're fine the way you're dressed," Andy said. "We'll get your abayas tomorrow afternoon when we go to the mall."

"Sabaah al-khair," Andy said to bus driver as the door opened. "Kayf haalak?"

"Sabaah al-noor. Tayyab[6]," said the driver.

---

[5] Saudi religious police charged with enforcing Sharia law.
[6] Good morning. How are you? (Response) Good morning. Fine.

"You're pretty good with that Arabic," I said to my smiling husband as Leis and I followed him into the diminutive bus.

After a brief ride down to the hospital, Andy led Leis and me to the auditorium half-filled with male expats, some wearing turbans, waiting for orientation to begin.

"As soon as this is over, we'll go to human resources," Andy said. "You'll have to hand over your passport to get the photo identification badge you'll need to go anywhere."

Day one of orientation began with the director of human resources giving guidelines for living and working on the self-contained, self-sustaining King Fahad National Guard Compound. More than 3,000 expats representing 37 different nationalities lived on compound and worked either at the hospital or a nearby facility that included a water-and-sewage system and an electrical power plant. The oval-shaped compound contained three unique areas separated by flat, open desert. King Fahad National Guard Hospital (KFNGH) was located at the west end of the compound. Medical City (MC), where employee apartments, recreation facilities, grocery store, restaurant and movie theater were located was in the middle. Medical City Extension (MCX) where our villa and others were located was at the east end of the compound. The entire compound was securely enclosed by a high concrete wall in some places or an electric barbed-wire fence in others, and accessible only through two heavily guarded entrances. Free, air-conditioned bus service ran between the hospital to MC to MCX every 15 minutes, around the clock.

The hospital's professional staff, including physicians, nurses and medical technicians were mostly Canadians, Americans, Europeans, Egyptians, Indians, Turkish Kurds, Syrians and Pakistanis. Service employees were mostly Filipinos, Bangladeshis, Yemenis and Sudanese, among other Asian and African nationalities. Professional staff lived in our neighborhood in MCX. Service staff personnel lived in barracks and apartments near MC.

Photography on the compound was strictly forbidden and punishable by deportation. No short shorts for men or women, only children. No bare arms for women and no two-piece bathing suits at the swimming pool during 'family time,' the only time married couples could swim together. Otherwise, it was 'males only' swimming. Leis and I were relieved to learn we did not have to wear veils out in the city. We were, however, required to wear an abaya, and a black headscarf if a mutawa ordered us to cover our hair.

Although married expat women were exempt, single female nurses employed at the hospital were required to sign out and in when leaving and re-entering the compound. Shopping buses left the compound at 8:30 a.m., 4:00 p.m. and 7:30 p.m. Buses returned to the compound at noon, 7:00 p.m. and 11:00 p.m.

Outside the compound, everyone had to obey the laws of Islam, Sharia law[7] (and the cultural dictates of Saudi Arabia) or risk being arrested, detained and/or deported.

Day one of orientation ended at 11:00. We went home for lunch and relaxed until we caught the shopping bus near our villa at 4:00 p.m. The shopping bus was a refurbished school bus twice the size of the compound bus, painted light blue and white, and owned and operated by King Fahad Hospital.

---

[7] The legal framework within which the public and some private aspects of life are regulated for those living in a legal system based on Islam.

With only two more stops, we were soon off compound and onto a six-lane highway. Cars, trucks and vehicles of every size and description whizzed by, switching lanes, blowing horns, determined to get there first, wherever they were headed. Our driver had shifted the bus into high gear, deftly merging into heavy traffic. The bus windows were open and the breeze felt good. A white, two-door Toyota shot by our window with a camel riding in the back. The camel appeared to be smiling. He was far less nervous than I felt going at such a high speed in such erratic traffic.

"Hang on tight," Andy said. He seemed to enjoy watching our first reactions to highway traffic in Riyadh, not for the fainthearted.

The shopping bus dropped us off at Al Aziziah Supermarket, popular with expatriates and similar in appearance to supermarkets back home. Our driver said he'd be back in an hour, before prayer time. With five prayer times throughout the day, shoppers planned accordingly. Everything came to a halt during prayer time and most shops and stores remained closed until prayer time was over. Some of the shops allowed expats to remain inside and continue shopping, although lights were dimmed and sales came to a halt. Familiar with time constraints while shopping, Andy quickly led us down the isles, filling our shopping cart as I crossed items off our list.

Many products on the shelves were recognizable brand names we could buy back home such as Jello, Kleenex, and Betty Crocker. Other items were complete mysteries with packaging all in Arabic. A meat counter offered fresh meats and poultry—more lamb than beef—and a variety of fresh fruits and vegetables, some familiar, some not, most imported from Jordan and Turkey. Peaches and fresh figs were exceptionally luscious and became among our favorite snacks. The dairy section offered all kinds of cheeses, yogurt, milk, including camel milk, and the Saudi version of sour cream or labnah, which I grew to love.

We bought enough staples to last a few days and made it out of the grocery before prayer time. We arrived home in time for a light dinner before heading down to the pool for a swim. We turned in early that night since we had to leave our villa at 6:45 to catch the seven o'clock compound bus back to the hospital.

On Sunday, day two of orientation, all hospital department heads gave a brief presentation on their area of expertise and responsibility. While several female physicians were in attendance, the only female who spoke was the supervisor of nursing; otherwise, all presenters were male. During our guided tour of the hospital, I was impressed by the cleanliness and state-of-the-art equipment. The entire hospital was on one floor, which meant no stairs or elevators and lots of walking.

With our identification badges in hand, Leis and I were free to explore the compound. I felt uneasy giving up my passport, something all expats were required to do. Andy did the same when he arrived in the Kingdom, exchanging his passport for an igama, a passport-like document similar to the U.S. green card. The Saudi igama gives an expat permission to live and work in Saudi Arabia. Since Leis and I were "dependents" on Andy's igama, we weren't issued our own. I understood how females in Saudi Arabia and other Middle Eastern countries could feel like 'chattel' or personal property with few rights of their own. For Western females, especially American women raised in a country and culture that values personal freedom, such restrictions were especially offensive.

I was beginning to understand some of the comments people made and concerns they had for me before we left for Saudi Arabia. Granted, cultural differences were extreme in some aspects of daily life, but I didn't come here to change the Saudis anymore than I expected my experience here to change my way of life once I was back home. I decided to embrace St. Ambrose's advice when he said, "When in Rome do as the Romans." I trusted Andy not to bring Leis and me to a place where we would be in danger, as long as we stayed within the law and respected local customs.

The last item on our to-do list that day was to take the shopping bus to Al-Shola Mall to buy abayas for Leis and me. Andy led the way up the stairs to a shop on the second level of the mall where abayas were available in every price range.

"I want the least expensive, most washable abaya I can find," I said, searching through the pile of black shrouds strewn across a large counter. "I don't need to make a fashion statement here. I'll *not* be wearing it back home."

"Here's one in polyester," said Leis, holding up what looked like a black shower curtain. We both settled for a plain abaya. Fancy ones with elaborate beading and embroidery could be purchased in upscale boutiques downtown—at much higher prices.

On Tuesday, July 4th, Andy proudly took possession of our white, 1989 Hyundai sedan with automatic transmission, power brakes and windows, air conditioning, a radio and tape player. Even though it was illegal for me to drive, I was grateful we had our own transportation.

"Happy Independence Day," Andy said, obviously pleased with his new purchase as he drove us out of the dealership.

"How ironic," I said, with a smile and a touch of sarcasm. "The freedoms I enjoyed back home, like driving a car and going where I want to go, are now forbidden to me."

After dinner that night, Andy asked Leis and me what we planned to do the next day since he would be back at work.

"Let's go to Olaya Mall," Leis said. "Just to look around."

I agreed with a twinge of reluctance. We would be on our own for the first time outside the compound without Andy to protect us.

Before we left the villa next morning, Leis and I wrapped ourselves in our abayas and made sure we had everything we'd need—sunglasses, water bottles, Saudi riyals, and identification badges clipped to our abayas. We were told only Muslim females beyond puberty were required to cover their heads. I dreaded the thought of being stopped by a mutawa so we each brought a black headscarf. I also brought the official, two-page document with Andy's, Leis's and my photos on it, verifying we were his dependents. When we left the villa at 8:20, the temperature outside was 90° F.

The shopping bus arrived on time and we were the first to board. At the next stop two blocks away, a tall, slim, attractive middle-aged woman with blond hair and a friendly smile boarded and sat across from us.

"Hello," she said. "You must be new here."

"Yes, we are," I said. "I'm Pam Daugavietis, and this is our daughter Leis. My husband Andy came to King Fahad Hospital in January. He's a rheumatologist. Leis and I arrived last week."

"Nice to meet you," she said as she held out her hand. "I'm Carol. My husband Martin is an anesthesiologist here. Martin said you were coming, but he wasn't sure when."

"How long have you lived here?"

"Almost seven months. We'll probably renew Martin's contract in the fall."

"Andy and I are here for two years," I said. "Leis lives in Florida with her mother so she'll be going home the first of August. Her brother

Peter will be coming July 17th for two weeks."

"Oh, how nice," said Carol. "Our son Chris will be here then, too. He's 20 and interested in computers. How old is Peter?"

"Nineteen in November."

"We'll get the boys together."

I felt a wave of excitement at the thought of having a friendship with this delightful woman who spoke with a slight British accent. She and her husband were from British Columbia. I liked her immediately.

Just then, our bus stopped again. A woman with three young girls boarded. The woman and the oldest girl wore abayas but no headscarves.

"Oh, good, here's Amina," said Carol, as she greeted her friend.

Amina was younger than Carol and I. She had short dark hair braided into a bun at the back of her head. She was tall, slim and attractive. Best of all, like Carol, she was upbeat and friendly.

"Hello and welcome, Pam and Leis," Amina said after Carol introduced us. "This is Ayesha, 12, Tahira, 9, and Farida, almost two. My husband Asiru is an endocrinologist at the hospital. We're Nigerian. We've been here a month."

I felt lucky to have new friends from two different countries. As a little girl growing up in a mostly conservative, white, Protestant Christian community in the Midwest, I never imagined I would be divorced and traveling to the Middle East with my second husband and stepdaughter. Being a 'new bride-to-be-the-second-time-around' was embarrassing, especially when meeting new friends for the first time, most with intact families. Having to explain the logistics of our fragmented family, and how Andy and I were here in Saudi Arabia without our kids felt awkward at times.

The shopping bus chugged along the highway at top speed, passing vehicles of all shapes and sizes. Once we left the highway, the bus slowed as we made our way into a neighborhood where the streets were lined with small shops. Pedestrians wearing Biblical-looking clothing crowded sidewalks. Women were covered in black and veiled. Men, some wearing turbans and some with shawls, wore loose-fitting gowns that looked like nightshirts. Shopkeepers selling hand-woven baskets, fresh produce, shoes and sandals, scarves and abayas, incense burners, brass trinkets and a variety of other items sat on their haunches sipping tea, looking up and down the sidewalk waiting for customers.

As we approached downtown, the sidewalks became wider, retail shops were larger and more modern looking, and numerous high-rise buildings were under construction. Construction cranes resembling huge, long-necked birds towered over every city block.

Our driver dropped us off in front of Olaya Mall, more modern looking than Al-Shola. Inside, we saw stores of every kind offering colorful fabric, women and children's clothing, perfume, books and stationery, shoes, spices and incense. Amina told us all sales clerks would be male, and it was illegal for females to remove their clothing in a store. If we wanted to try something on, we had to go to the female public toilets. Otherwise, buy the item, bring it home and return it next day if it's not suitable. Another option was to buy fabric. Carol told me if I wanted a dress, skirt, blouse or jacket made, she knew an excellent tailor who charged reasonable prices.

We agreed to meet Carol and Amina and the girls at 11:30 at the bus stop and waved goodbye. They had specific shopping to do, and Leis and I just wanted to look around. In addition to retail shops, the mall included a pharmacy, a bakery and a grocery store. All signs were in Arabic, although once in a while a sign would also be in English. A dry cleaning shop had an amusing translation (at least to us English-speaking expats) that read: "Drop your pants here."

Some stores posted a sign, in large, black lettering, in Arabic and English, *"No women allowed!"* Leis and I stopped to look in the front window of a video store where such a sign was prominently displayed. A Filipino male standing inside the door saw us and hurried out.

"Ma'am, if you want to enter, it okay. Mafee mushkala[8]. No mutawa 'til afternoon. After prayer time."

We shook our heads and continued down the mall. After an hour or so of window-shopping, Leis said she was thirsty and wanted something besides water to drink. I had seen a Dairy Queen around the corner, so we backtracked and walked through the front entrance. We passed a booth filled with teenage Saudi males who started laughing and pointing at us.

"Ignore them," I whispered to Leis as we walked to the counter by the cash register. When the man behind the counter saw us, he gasped as if we were ghosts. An armed guard came out of nowhere and rushed toward us waving his arms and shouting.

"La, la, la, la[9]," he said, his face twisted in a scowl as he pointed to a cordoned off area in the corner of the shop. With his other hand, he motioned for us to go there, *immediately*. It took me a nanosecond to realize what we had done. I placed my hands on Leis's shoulders and pointed her toward the family section.

"Over there, Leis," I said. "I'm right behind you. Don't look at those guys."

---

[8] No problem.
[9] No, no, no, no!

We turned away from the counter, holding our heads high. As we passed our detractors, I glanced down and caught a glimpse of their grinning faces. I resisted a motherly urge to stop and scold these ignorant youths for their rudeness. Instead, we made our way through the heavy, maroon-colored curtains into the family section and ordered our drinks. A young, veiled Saudi mother and her toddler were eating ice cream at another table. Leaving through the family-section entrance, we spotted Carol and Amina and the girls at the other end of the mall. We hurried to catch up with them, eager to tell about our first cultural gaffe.

"At first I was startled and then angry that Leis and I were treated so rudely," I said. "I'm happy to obey the rules around here but some are absurd."

"Don't judge Islam by how it's practiced in Saudi Arabia," said Amina, a devout Muslim. "True Islam is a religion of love and tolerance. Here, cultural tradition limits the status of females. It's not like this in other parts of the world."

That evening, Andy drove us downtown to the gold souks, an open area filled with countless stalls selling gold jewelry. Overhead track lights throughout the market made the 18- and 24-karat gold jewelry sparkle and shine to entice customers. Male shopkeepers weighed jewelry in scales to determine the price according to the price of gold on the international market. Shopkeepers expected buyers to bargain. Savvy customers knew better than to buy at the first price offered.

There only to look, we simply strolled up and down the aisles, stopping occasionally to admire the endless assortment of earrings, bracelets and necklaces. Many expats were away on summer vacation, so we Americans were in the minority among many Saudis and other Middle

Easterners shoppers. At one stall, I noticed the Saudi shopkeeper looking at Leis, admiring her white skin and long blond hair.

"She your daughter?" the shopkeeper asked Andy.

"Yes," Andy said, more interested in the gold on display than in the shopkeeper's question.

"I give you 100 camels for her."

"Not enough," Andy said, glancing up at the young man eying his daughter.

"One hundred Mercedes."

"You're getting close," Andy said, smiling, as he herded Leis and me out of the shop.

Chapter 3

A Dream Come True

We were all looking forward to Peter's visit—especially Leis. She was eager to show him around the compound and take him downtown on the shopping bus. In two weeks, they would return to the U.S. I was looking forward to Peter's visit, too, thankful Leis would have someone to spend time with. She and I had been on the go since we arrived almost a month earlier. Andy and I needed time alone as a couple. We'd been legally married since January and still not had a honeymoon or time to talk, shop, cook, socialize with other couples or simply spend a quiet evening at home, alone, together.

As much as I cared for Leis and Peter, I was missing John and Bob—a lot. The reality of being in a blended family was beginning to sink in. Throughout the day I'd think about my boys, how they were doing and what they were doing. The red tape required for visitors' visas for non-Saudis who were not dependents of expats with igamas was too complicated to arrange. John and Bob weren't Andy's dependents so it was impossible for them to visit. I had chosen to come to Saudi Arabia with Andy, a decision I never regretted. Still, I was painfully aware I was missing Bob's last years of high school and John's first years in college.

At times, I'd feel jealous of Bridget. I knew I should be grateful she was taking good care of the boys. I wanted to be a loving stepmother to Peter and Leis, but they already had a mother. Did Pat ever feel jealous of me, the way I sometimes felt about Bridget?

I didn't feel comfortable sharing my feelings and emotions with Leis even though we had a close relationship. Mature beyond her years, Leis was still a teenager. I didn't tell Andy how I felt because I didn't want him to think I was having second thoughts about our marriage and living in Saudi Arabia, because I wasn't.

Calling Mother for a long talk wasn't an option. With limited phone lines, a line wasn't always available when you wanted to call. Phoning the U.S. from Saudi Arabia was more expensive than phoning Saudi Arabia from the U.S. The eight-hour time difference made calls more challenging to arrange.

Instead, I wrote letters to Mother expressing my homesickness and feelings of ambiguity. I loved Andy and was happy to be his wife, yet I missed John and Bob. Getting these feelings and emotions out of my head and heart and down on paper was an enormous relief. For me, writing was the next best thing to talking to my mother on the phone. Her letters back to me were my comfort.

"Your feelings are normal, Pammy, considering all the changes you've had to adjust to lately," she wrote with her usual wisdom. "You're doing fine. Don't worry about the boys. They're fine, too."

Although Carol, Amina and I had visited together a few times since we met, I still didn't feel comfortable sharing my feelings with them. Neither of them was divorced, although Amina's two older daughters were Asiru's from a previous marriage. Only Farida, the youngest, was their child together. The reality was that most couples we knew had their own younger children living with them, or older children back home in boarding school or living independently in another country. Expat families were accustomed to living apart from their children, at least some of the time. Being so far away from my boys was a new and challenging experience for me. Thankfully, they had both called several times and assured me they were doing well. My two sisters and my mother took turns calling on weekends and Andy's parents called regularly, too. I deeply appreciated all their calls because I knew they were expensive. Yet, I couldn't live from phone call to phone call from home for the next year and a half to help ease my homesickness and culture shock.

I soon realized that keeping house for just the two of us, interspersed with occasional shopping trips and lunches with other expat wives, wasn't enough to keep me busy and content all week. Yet, I had no expectations of finding a job in Saudi Arabia that appealed to me.

The afternoon before Peter arrived, Andy called from the hospital, something he rarely, if ever, had the time or opportunity to do.

"How would you like to be a media specialist in the hospital's Public Affairs Department?"

"What's a media specialist?"

"Not sure," he said. "Call Mohammed Al Senaidy at extension 5367. He's expecting you."

"What do you mean he's expecting me? Have you been talking with him on my behalf?

"I didn't want to tell you but I approached him a week or so ago. I told him about your interests and experience and that you were a writer and wanted to work. He said he was interested in hiring you but wasn't sure if Administration would approve another writer for his department. He's called four or five times to remind me to call Human Resources to put in a good word for you."

"Well, did you?"

"Of course."

My dear husband knew about my passion for writing, although I had never made it a career. He also knew job opportunities for females in Saudi Arabia were limited. Most Saudi females were expected to marry young and birth many children, often sharing their husband's attention and affection with other wives. Nursing and teaching were the most popular career choices for Saudi females who chose to get an education and have a career outside the home. While I came to Saudi Arabia as Andy's wife and not necessarily to work, I hoped to at least keep my brain engaged and my mind occupied with something interesting and worthwhile. A job as a real writer would be a dream come true.

That afternoon, when I called Mr. Al Senaidy, he was busy so I spoke with his assistant, Nabiha, a young Jordanian woman.

"The position you're inquiring about has not been approved by Human Resources," Nabiha said. "Mr. Al Senaidy is hopeful he'll hear from them this week. Still, he would like to see you tomorrow for a preliminary interview if you're available."

"Is there anything I need to know about the position of media specialist before I meet with Mr. Al Senaidy, like what it entails?"

"Candidates must be bilingual in English and Arabic."

"I only speak English. My Arabic classes don't start until next week."

"Don't worry about it," she said. "No big deal. You'll be fine."

I hadn't met Nabiha face-to-face but I liked her immediately and took her at her word. She scheduled a meeting between Mr. Al Senaidy and me for 11:00 the next morning. Peter's plane arrived shortly before midnight. He wasn't bothered by jet lag and was ready to go exploring next morning. After Andy left for work, Peter, Leis and I took the shuttle bus to the hospital to get Peter's identification badge. From there, we parted ways. Peter and Leis headed for the pool. I went to my first job interview.

"Welcome, Mrs. Daugavietis," said Mr. Al Senaidy without extending his hand. His warmth and enthusiasm put me at ease. "Please come in and meet Abdullah, my assistant."

Mr. Al Senaidy was about my height and perhaps a few years older. He wore tinted glasses and had prominent dark eyebrows, a dark, bushy mustache and a wide smile. All Saudi men wore white thobes and red and white checkered ghutras or headscarves, and all wore mustaches or some kind of facial hair. Amina told me Muslim males grow facial hair to indicate their devotion to their Islamic faith—the longer and more unkempt the beard, the more traditional and pious the man.

Abdullah, who was younger than Mr. Al Senaidy, did not extend his hand, nor did he look me in the eye or smile. He lowered his eyes and bowed slightly. Mr. Al Senaidy motioned for me to take a chair across from his desk, next to Abdullah's chair.

"How's your husband?" he asked.

"Fine, fine," I said, thinking his question a strange way to begin a job interview. Perhaps it was because Andy had first approached him about a job for me and he wanted to show respect. He said he was impressed by my educational background and wanted to know more about my work experience, like which job listed I liked best.

"I love writing inspiring stories about real people," I said. "When I worked for the Ohio Department of Health, I interviewed migrant children and families who benefitted from health care provided in community clinics."

Mr. Al Senaidy said nothing. He kept nodding and reading my résumé. Abdullah seemed more interested in my impressions of King Fahad Hospital and how I liked living in Saudi Arabia than in my credentials.

"What do you think about the hospital? Abdullah said.

"It's beautiful, very modern. Employees are friendly and helpful."

I tried to keep my remarks as complimentary as possible, assuring them I would be pleased and proud to become a member of the Public Affairs staff. While I sensed the interview went well, I had little hope of landing the job because of the Arabic requirement. No way would I learn to speak Arabic in a few weeks. By American standards, the salary they were offering was low, but in the Middle East, for females, Andy said it was okay. All our living expenses except food were included in Andy's contract, so my income covered extras and incidentals. I was fortunate and I knew it, compared to workers from developing countries who put in long hours for low pay.

I decided to enjoy the kids' visit and worry later about how to keep myself busy if the job at the hospital didn't work out. After Andy got home from work, the four of us drove downtown for shawarmas and fruit drinks, our favorite Saudi 'fast food'. A shawarma is shaved beef, chicken, lamb or fish wrapped in Arabic or pita flatbread, along with a few sweet pickles, several French-fried potatoes covered with a distinctly flavored mayonnaise-like sauce. My favorite was chicken; Andy loved chicken and lamb. One shawarma was all I could eat; Andy could eat two. They weren't large in size, but greasy, filling, and delicious. The popular fruit drink made with pineapple juice, strawberries and bananas blended together with ice was a refreshing accompaniment to the shawarma.

~

Now into the second week of Peter's visit, Andy and I, Peter and Leis set out on our first weekend road trip—to Al Jubail, a large oil port and refinery on the Arabian Gulf[10]. Weekends in Saudi Arabia began on Thursday with Friday being their holy day[11]. Thus, the four of us set out by car on a Wednesday evening after Andy came home from the hospital, eager for a new adventure.

Thankfully, Andy knew to arrange for written approval from human resources to make the trip by car. Two uniformed policemen stopped us at a police checkpoint on the outskirts of Riyadh. They looked over Andy's papers and searched our car, even under the seats. Satisfied that we weren't carrying contraband, they motioned for us to continue our travels. The four-and-a-half-hour drive across the desert was uneventful. Signs along the highway warned us to watch for camels, like watching for deer back home in Michigan. Occasionally, we spotted groups of camels and sheep grazing at a distance, although we didn't know what they were grazing on. It was nothing but desert in all directions. We did encounter one lonely camel walking along the highway in the opposite direction on our side of the road, apparently lost from the herd.

Al Jubail turned out to be relaxing and fun but more hot and humid than Riyadh. Our saving grace was central air conditioning in the hotel. On the beach, cool breezes from the Arabian Gulf provided some relief from temperatures hovering around 115° Fahrenheit in the direct sun.

Leis and I were required to wear one-piece bathing suits. Andy and Peter wore traditional men's swimming trunks. We covered ourselves with the soft and luxurious terrycloth robes that came with our room. Walking single file from our hotel through a path of tall grass, the four of us found

---

[10] In the 1960s, when the rivalry between Iran and some of the Arab nations escalated, the Saudis changed the name of the Persian Gulf to the Arabian Gulf.

[11] In 2013, Saudi Arabia officially changed their two-day weekend to begin on a Friday, which remains their holy day. Their workweek now begins on Sunday, so their workdays overlap by four days, rather than three, with other countries in their region and around the world to make trade and business transactions easier.

our way to a small inlet of water, cordoned off for swimming. After we arranged our beach chairs and belongings under our cabana, Andy and Peter went straight to the water's edge. Leis and I sat down to assess the situation before taking off our sunglasses and robes. We looked across the open beach to the other side of the small inlet of blue water to where four Saudi females were sitting in chairs like ours, all dressed in black—from head to foot. Three Saudi adult males and seven or eight young boys and girls, all dressed in Western-style bathing suits, splashed and played in the water, tossing a huge beach ball back and forth. Out in the middle of this small inlet of water, four more adult females, completely covered in black, veils and all, were paddling around in a four-seat paddleboat.

"I want to go in the water, but I don't want to take off my robe," I said to Leis. "I think those females are staring at us. I'm self-conscious in a one-piece when they're covered in black."

"Come on in, the water's great," Andy called out to us as he stood bare-chested and knee deep in sparkling blue water, grinning from ear to ear. He was unfazed by the cultural discrepancies that Leis and I found embarrassing. Peter was already out into the deeper part of the lagoon, enjoying relief from the heat. Leis and I mustered enough courage to drop our robes and walk briskly to the water's edge. I lunged forward, trying to submerge myself as quickly as possible without hitting my chin on the bottom. I wondered what the Saudi females were thinking of us half-naked Western females splashing around in the water while they sat covered in black in this unbearable heat. Did they regard us as brazen women? I rolled over on my back, sat up, then quickly retreated to the cabana, content to hide behind my sunglasses and under my robe, sip water and relax until Andy and the kids were ready to leave.

On the last night of our stay in Al Jubail, we splurged by dining in the hotel's five-star restaurant. The *maître d'* seated us in a round booth under a tent-like enclosure surrounded by heavy drapery except for an opening so the male wait-staff could serve our food. With all tables 'tented' for privacy, we could see only one other couple dining closest to our table. When servers arrived with more food, the curtains parted long enough for us to see inside. The Saudi male wore the traditional thobe and ghutra. His wife was veiled and completely covered in black, including black gloves. Leis and I were more than curious to know how she managed to eat. We tried to peer discretely through the opening of our 'tent' to see her delicately lifting the edge of her veil with one hand while bringing a fork full of food to her mouth with the other.

      After returning to our villa on Friday evening, we had one day to do laundry and get Peter and Leis packed and ready to go back to the U.S. Sunday night. Peter would go with Leis to Tallahassee for two weeks before returning to Michigan to begin his freshman year at the University of Michigan. Leis would begin her senior year at Leon High School in Tallahassee. John would be a junior at Hillsdale College and Bob would be a senior at Petoskey High School. After Peter and Leis left, Andy and I settled into a predictable and enjoyable routine. Carol and Amina and I went shopping together during the day and met for lunch at the MC restaurant. I enjoyed having time alone in our villa to read and write letters back home. Andy and I did grocery shopping on weekends and planned our weekly menus. In spite of missing the boys and waiting to get word about the job in Public Affairs, I felt more settled and content than I had in months. I should have known this near idyllic, 'honeymoon' phase of our mid-life adventure wouldn't last long.

Chapter 4

The 'Magic' Kingdom

My Arabic classes at the hospital on Saturday and Tuesday mornings gave me something to do while waiting to hear from Public Affairs. Gabir, our teacher, was a tall, soft-spoken Sudanese man with a warm smile and dazzling white teeth. Deep tribal scars on either side of his wide nose were healed but conspicuous on his dark skin. I didn't speak Arabic well enough to ask him how old he was when he was cut like that, or why. I was also uncertain if such a question from a Western female was improper so I never asked. With eight English-speaking students in our group, we were learning spoken Arabic rather than classical Arabic or even modern written Arabic. Our goal was not to read Arabic but to communicate on an elementary level. Gabir was a patient man, always encouraging. Even simple spoken Arabic was difficult for many of us in the class so our progress was slow. Yet, he continually encouraged and praised us for our gradual improvement, word-by-word and phrase-by-phrase.

On Monday morning, one week into my Arabic classes, the phone rang unusually early. My first thought was an emergency at home so I was relieved when the caller identified himself as Nasir Siddiqi, from Human Resources.

"Oh, yes, Mr. Siddiqi. I was hoping to hear from you."

"Your position has been approved. Are you available to attend a brief orientation Sunday morning at 11: 00?"

"Yes, I'm available."

"Good, Mrs. Daugavietis, good. Mr. Al Senaidy reported that your interview with him went well. I carefully reviewed your résumé and application, and everything is in fine order. We've never had an English-speaking writer on staff and we're lucky to have someone with your experience. Your first day of work is August 26th. Please report to Nabiha at 8:00 a.m."

I couldn't wait to tell Andy the good news.

"Thanks for getting me a writing job at the hospital," I said, wrapping my arms around him as he walked in the door that night.

"I didn't get you a job, you got it yourself."

"Yes, you did, and you know it. Mr. Siddiqi said they were lucky to have me."

"Well, they are."

I had great expectations of a new career ahead of me. Even in Saudi Arabia, I could continue to work on my writing skills, moving me closer to my lifelong dream of being a *real* writer.

That evening, after supper and prayer time, Andy and I drove downtown to pick up our new computer. No longer would I have to write letters longhand. We also stopped in Batha, a popular shopping area in Riyadh, to pick up the double-strand pearl necklace the Bedouin ladies made for me. I bought the pearls and had the necklace made with going-away gift money from my Petoskey friends.

That night, I lay in bed thinking about my boys and wondering what they were doing. I thought about my mother, my sisters, other family members and friends back home. I missed them all, especially John and Bob, but life on King Fahad Hospital compound *was* getting better.

~

As a hospital employee, I was required to undergo a complete physical exam including blood tests, urinalysis, eye exam, hearing exam, chest x-ray and electrocardiogram. After my lab tests were completed, I made an appointment with a female family practice physician, born and raised in Australia, now from Toronto, Canada. I was grateful to be seen by a female physician, one I immediately felt comfortable with when we first met, especially because of my embarrassing bladder condition of not always being able to "go" when in a hurry or in a public restroom. She was a few years older than I, and married with two sons who were both attending college in Toronto.

"Doctor, my urologist back home in Petoskey told me I had paruresis[12], an inability to urinate in public," I said. "He told me I was born with *spina bifida occulta*, which caused the condition. He prescribed disposable catheters for me to use intermittently—only when needed. I have to be careful to avoid urinary tract infections."

"Pam, call me Judith," she said reassuringly. "Yes, I'm aware of this problem and I sympathize with you. However, toilets for females in Saudi Arabia, and even throughout Europe, are quite private."

"I've noticed," I said. "This was a welcome discovery."

My Petoskey doctor told me some who have paruresis become homebound, afraid to travel or be away from home for a long time. Determined not to let this happen to me, I'd quit drinking liquids a day before a long flight and I'd use every private restroom I came across, whether I had to 'go' or not. So far, my strategy had worked fairly well.

I told Judith about Andy giving several of my antibiotic capsules

---

[12] Studies show that approximately 7% of the U.S. population or 21 million people, may suffer from paruresis. (www.paruresis.org)

to a young Saudi female on our flight to Riyadh because of her urinary tract infection. She prescribed another antibiotic she said might be more effective since I only took them occasionally and not every day. I thanked her for her understanding, sensitivity and helpful advice. Even though Andy's specialty wasn't urology, he was patient and understanding of my condition. I could never have come so far away from home without him. With no other comments from Dr. Judith regarding my state of wellness, I was ready to go to work.

~

My big day finally arrived. I rode down to the hospital with Andy at 7:00 a.m. and reported to Nabiha in Public Affairs.

"Welcome, Pam," she said warmly. "Good to have you here."

Nabiha's smile disappeared and she lowered her gaze.

"Sorry to tell you, we have no more space in the department. Your office is in Ward 16. Helen, the head nurse, is expecting you. Mr. Al Senaidy will meet with you soon."

I made my way down the long, narrow hallway to huge double doors marked Ward 16. Helen was the only one sitting behind the nurses' station.

"Welcome to the *Magic* Kingdom," she said with a smirk-like smile, slightly lifting her right eyebrow.

"'*Magic* Kingdom'?" I asked. "What do you mean?"

"You'll find out soon enough," she said as she stood up and extended her hand.

Helen was Canadian—slim, short brown hair, mid 20s—and wore a white nurse's uniform, white shoes and hose, but no white cap. She was all business, telling—not asking—a nearby staff nurse to watch the phone while she stepped away for a minute. Motioning for me to follow, Helen strode ahead of me down the hall a short distance, opened the door to my new office and stepped aside so I could enter first.

"This was a storage closet, then a collection site for hazardous materials," she said, giving me another wry smile. "They cleaned it up just for you."

Once inside the windowless 12' by 16' cubicle brightly lit with ceiling lights, I was stunned by what I saw. Three large, metal desks dominated the tiny room, all crammed together with one desk against the far wall. Clearly, the person sitting at the far desk was trapped if either of the other two desks were occupied. Just as I was about to ask who 'they' were to arrange the room in such a manner, two Saudi males appeared at the door. One of them was Abdullah I met in Mr. Al Senaidy's office the day of my interview. Both wore thobes and ghutras, pagers clipped to one side pocket and prayer beads[13] dangling from the other. Falah introduced himself and Abdullah as assistants to Mr. Al Senaidy. Falah smiled and was more animated than Abdullah, who didn't smile or look us in the eye when he spoke.

"How do you like your new office, Missus Pamela Daugavietis?" Abdullah said, waving his hand around the room with a grand gesture.

"Abdullah and I arranged everything," Falah said proudly. "All by ourselves."

Helen shot me another amusing smile.

"Thank you, both," I said. "I'm sure I'll love it."

Two females appeared at the door. Ignoring the newcomers, Falah and Abdullah excused themselves and left. Hala, the younger and livelier of the two, introduced herself and Suhair as my new office mates.

---

[13] Prayer beads are used by members of various religions to mark repetitions of prayers or devotions. In Islam, the beads represent prayers to God or Allah. All Saudi males carry them.

Suhair, silent and somber until now, looked at me and smiled. "We're Egyptian, not Saudi," she said quietly.

Only Suhair wore the traditional headscarf worn by female Muslims. Both Hala and Suhair were bi-lingual in Arabic and English. When they saw how Falah and Abdullah had arranged our office, they scoffed.

"No surprise," said Hala, shaking her head in disgust. "Typical male pride."

"Always taking credit for nothing," said Suhair in a low, almost inaudible voice, hands clasped at her waist.

Before lunchtime that day, Suhair, Hala and I rearranged the desks with the help of several Filipino servers on Ward 16. Space was tight but at least it was workable.

That afternoon, Mr. Al Senaidy called me into his office to give me my first writing assignment. Reaching for a handful of dates in a large bowl on the edge of his desk, he ate one after the other, spitting pits into his other hand and tossing them into a nearby wastebasket.

"Help yourself," he said, smiling broadly, pointing to the empty straight-backed chair across from his desk.

"No thank you," I said, as I sat down with pen in hand and my notepad on my lap.

"How's your husband?" he said.

"Fine, fine. I'll tell him you asked about him." I wondered how long such chitchat was supposed to last, definitely a Saudi custom and not a Western one. I quickly learned that Western expats, when they first came to the hospital as employees, tended to be impatient and demanding. Saudis were more easygoing and conversational, a charming trait at times but frustrating at others.

"That's good, that's good," he said, as he reached for another date.

"And my assignment?" I said, eager to have something to occupy my thoughts and feelings besides homesickness and boredom.

"Your first assignment is to attend the graduation ceremony for the second annual King Fahad National Guard Hospital Summer Program. It will be held day after tomorrow in the auditorium at 1:00. We need a press release by noon for the *Arab News,* and an article later on for *The Bulletin,* our monthly magazine. You'll be able to interview several graduates at the event. Tomorrow, Nabiha will have your official white coat and a Public Affairs identification badge. You're required to wear both at all times during work hours."

~

I couldn't wait for the *Arab News* to come out the following Sunday. I wanted to see the article about the graduation ceremony. When I walked into my office, the morning edition was lying face up on my desk. A front-page headline read: *Hospital Program Trainees Get Diplomas, By K.S. Ramkumar, Arab News Staff.* I read the entire article, much of it word for word from my news release. Something important was missing. Where was the item about the young female graduate I interviewed? She inspired me because she broke tradition as a female by studying to become a medical-surgical physician. I interviewed both a male and female graduate that day. The item about the male graduate was included; the item about the female graduate wasn't. I hurried down the hallway from my office to Public Affairs to see Mr. Al Senaidy.

"Why did they leave out the item about Wafaa Banaser?" I said, showing him the front page of the paper. "I told her to watch for the article. I found her story to be quite inspiring."

"The editorial committee didn't find it interesting," he said, momentarily looking up at me from his desk. He didn't speak rudely, but in a way that made it clear the matter was closed. He went back to his reading.

Salah appeared at the door. "Pam, come to my office."

Salah was younger than Mr. Al Senaidy. He didn't have Mr. Al Senaidy's level of authority, but he sometimes acted that way. I liked Salah in spite of his tendency at times to seem arrogant and condescending. His braggadocios manner may have been more of an attempt to make a good first impression rather than his real personality. When I walked into his office, he looked grim. I wondered if he was about to reprimand me for writing about the female medical student. At least I hadn't included the fact that the female graduates weren't allowed to walk across the stage that day to get their diplomas, and the fact they had to wait *behind* male graduates for refreshments after the ceremony.

"Pam, we want you to be the English editor of *The Bulletin*," Salah said to my utter surprise. "We need someone with excellent English skills to review the English portion of the magazine. You don't have to answer right away. Think about it. Talk to your husband, but let me know soon."

The Bulletin was the hospital's full-color, monthly, 16-page magazine for employees. The first half of the magazine was written in English and the second half, identical to the first half, was written in Arabic.

"Thank you, Salah, for your confidence in me," I said, trying to conceal my excitement. "I'll think about it this evening, discuss it with my husband, and let you know my answer tomorrow."

If I had said 'yes' right away, which I was inclined to do, I would have made the offer seem less important than Salah felt it was. Plus, I would be leaving out the most important consideration: my husband's approval. I was learning the subtleties of proper communication with Saudi males in the work environment. My self-confidence soared knowing my skills were needed and appreciated. It also felt empowering for Salah to ask me to take on such a responsibility. *This must mean they respect me and trust me to do a good job*—or so I assumed.

I took the August issue of *The Bulletin* home that night to read it carefully. I soon discovered an English editor was needed for more than spelling and grammar. In the *Face From The Hospital,* an interview with plastic surgeon Dr. Pitkanen listed his photograph, name, marital status, qualifications and degrees (all with meaningless abbreviations and acronyms), work experience, position and date of hire. Next were a series of mindless questions followed by Dr. Pitkanen's answers: "Your philosophy in dealing with sons (firm but understanding), friends (come and go but enemies accumulate - cf. Murphy's law), superiors (cooperative but if necessary, critical), employees (social and disciplined); Most interesting happening you have ever encountered (met a shark while diving); Your Favorite Hobby (sailing and photography); Country you would like to visit and never seen before (Iceland); Last Book you read (The lost war [sic])."

Other sections in the August issue included *Departmental News, For Your Health, Kingdom of Saudi Arabia, Yesterday and Today, Islamic Culture, For Your Information* and finally, *This Makes Me Laugh.* Most everything I read in the English section made me laugh.

A sampling of articles that especially caught my attention: *The Status of Women in Islam* and *Sneezing Can Improve Your Complexion.*

The Status of Women in Islam explained why females in Saudi Arabia veil when in public or with males who are not their husbands.

> *The Muslim woman is always associated with an old tradition known as the "veil." It is Islamic that the (sic) women should beautify herself with the veil of honor, dignity, chastity, purity and integrity. She should refrain from all deeds and gestures that might*

> *stir the passions of people other than her legitimate husband or cause evil suspicion of her morality. She is warned not to display her charms or expose her physical attractions before strangers. Islam is most concerned with the integrity of woman (sic), with the safeguarding of her morals and with the protection of her character and personality. By now it is clear that the status of woman (sic) in Islam is unprecedentedly high and realistically suitable to her nature.*

The article about the benefits of sneezing reveals a surprising outcome of "recent research." Allegedly, sneezing 15 minutes a day for two weeks helps remove acne and other facial blemishes by tightening the pores. Dermatology wasn't Andy's specialty but when I asked him about this claim he said it was absurd.

A cartoon in the *This Makes Me Laugh* section showed a bearded man wearing glasses pointing to a circular pie chart with 'OK' in the 10 percent and 'DUMB' in the 90 percent with this caption: "Thomas's Theory On The Composition of the Universe—90% of everything is stupid." This attempt at humor didn't seem an appropriate way to build confidence with staff or patient population of a tertiary hospital, all hoping for positive outcomes. One could imagine a Saudi and an expat laughing at the same joke for different reasons because of different interpretations.

As time went on, I better understood Helen's comment: "Welcome to the *Magic* Kingdom."

My official job description stated I was to "coordinate the flow of information to the public, the hospital community and the Saudi Arabian National Guard, using a variety of media sources."

My principal duties were to "write and edit articles emphasizing the best points of the hospital to the public; keep the public informed of the latest events about the hospital itself, through writing to all media channels, i.e. TV, newspapers, radio, etc."

It all sounded good on paper but the reality was I never had the authority to make more important decisions about content, scheduling, design and production. I gradually realized Salah wanted me to review spelling and grammar only, rather than oversee editorial content and production. Reluctantly, I accepted the position of English editor of *The Bulletin,* with the hope that eventually, I would prove my worth to Salah and Mr. Al Senaidy by improving the content and relevance of *The Bulletin* for Western readers as well as Arabic speaking readers. Time would tell.

Chapter 5

Honeymoon in Turkey

When Andy suggested Turkey as a honeymoon destination, I winced. Turkey didn't sound very romantic to me. Granted, I knew little about the country, its religion, culture and history. My interest was roused when Andy said we could attend church together in Istanbul and enjoy a glass of wine with dinner. When he said I could leave my abaya at home and hold his hand in public without fearing mutawa, my resistance eased. He went on to describe the heart-healthy Mediterranean cuisine, the music, temperate weather and numerous historical sites. Soon, I was convinced Turkey would be perfect. Although Andy had never been there himself, he had heard colleagues say it was their favorite holiday destination.

For Andy, getting time off was not a problem. American and Canadian physicians enjoyed generous paid-vacation days. When I spoke with Mr. Al Senaidy about time off to go to Turkey, he was reluctant. I had been on the job only a month. When I told him it was our honeymoon and I didn't expect to be paid while away, he agreed to let me leave. I worked diligently, conducting interviews and writing several articles ahead so my absence wouldn't affect deadlines for *The Bulletin*.

On the morning of our departure, we were eager to leave. We stood by the back door with our two suitcases waiting for the limousine driver to arrive. Punctuality wasn't part of the Saudi culture so we always arranged for pick-up earlier than needed in case of a delay. The weather was perfect—

sunny and 82° Fahrenheit. Riyadh weather was hot, never humid. Excited and grateful to be leaving Saudi Arabia for 14 days to a country with fewer cultural restrictions, we were elated when our driver pulled up on time.

Our travels from Riyadh to Jeddah and from Jeddah to Istanbul went smoothly. During our flights, we sipped wine and scanned travel books, trying to decide what to see first. Landing late afternoon, we made our way through the terminal to the information counter to inquire about hotels. We hadn't made prior arrangements for hotels as recommended by Andy's contacts. In a directory at the airport, we found an affordable hotel, made a reservation via phone, and caught a taxi for the 30-minute drive into the heart of the old city.

"So . . . . this is . . . . *Istanbul*?" I said, peering out the taxi's backseat windows. We drove through block after block of deteriorating buildings in crowded neighborhoods darkened by time and neglect. I don't know what I expected, but what I was seeing didn't look like the photos I saw in travel books of this ancient yet modern metropolis.

Even though our hotel was advertised as "Istanbul's best at a reasonable price," our accommodations were not up to Western standards. Our fourth-floor room with adjoining bathroom was clean but diminutive. The bathroom sink and tub were stained. Several tiles on the floor and walls were cracked and a few were missing. The bed, desk and two chairs were worn and outdated. The room's one large, double window was open with no screen, exposing our room to dust and noise from the street. I walked to the window and saw a man wearing nothing but undershorts, standing in a hotel room across the street, looking down at the sidewalk below while smoking a cigarette. I fell to my knees, crawled to the end of the window and pulled down the shades.

"I don't know about this place," I said to Andy, who was surprised to see me crawling on all fours as he came out of the bathroom.

We cleaned up a bit and set out to find a place to eat. Our hotel clerk, who spoke little English, motioned for us to follow him out to the sidewalk. He pointed in the direction we should go. It was early evening and getting dark. We thought we were going in the right direction when we turned down a dimly lit alley. Halfway down, we found ourselves wading through garbage. We kept a tight grip on each other in case one of us fell. This was not just a few papers and discarded bits of food here and there. We were up to our ankles in solid garbage, lettuce leaves and tomatoes, pieces of bread and other food scraps, paper towels, empty cans, bottles, cigarette butts, an assortment of cardboard containers. We saw a lighted crossroad down the way so we hurried as best we could without mishap.

Moments later we came to an open area, well lit and crowded with couples walking hand in hand, some women in abayas and headscarves but no veil, some tourists wearing western-style clothing, a refreshing mix of cultures. Distinctive Turkish music, along with happy chatter and laughter filled the air. The mood on the street was celebratory, perhaps for no other reason than it was dinnertime. Aromas coming from open-window restaurants along the walkway were tempting. Quickly, we found a place that suited us, the Yelken Balik Restaurant, where we enjoyed swordfish and a bottle of 1985 sec dry Turkish wine from Ismir. Walking back to our hotel, we passed the same alley now cleared of debris. We had walked through the alley right after the market closed, before the cleanup crew arrived.

At dawn the next morning, we were awakened by the call to prayer coming from the mosque half a block away. That, and our bathroom being so small you had to sit on the toilet to brush your teeth over the sink, caused us to look for another hotel. After breakfast, we packed our bags and carried them five or six blocks to Hotel Gulsoy. In truth, the two hotels were much the same—small and outdated but the man at the front desk welcomed us warmly. After checking into our second-floor room, we came out onto the sidewalk to get our bearings. The city was alive with noise and activity—pedestrians crossing the street every which way, heavy vehicle traffic vying for room to pass, horns honking, sea gulls soaring overhead against a bright, blue sky. Andy opened a huge map of the city to see where we were in this confusing mix of humanity. I looked over his shoulder as I clutched my large woven Nigerian bag (popular with Western expats) to my chest. Our camera was hanging from a leather strap around my neck. It couldn't have been more obvious to anyone spotting us that we were inexperienced tourists.

"May I be of service?" a male voice said in perfect English.

Standing before us was a dark-haired, middle-aged fellow with a wide smile and generous mustache. He was smartly dressed in a Western-style, dark suit with his white shirt unbuttoned at the top, no tie. He reached for his wallet and flipped it open for a nanosecond to reveal his photo identification card, hardly long enough to read the fine print.

"My name is Ahmet Faruk Haksoyleyen," he said, extending his hand to both of us. "I'm a reporter for the Turkish Press, native of Istanbul, tour guide, a *private* tour guide—with my own car and driver. May I have the honor of showing you around Istanbul, for a modest fee, of course?"

"What do you think?" Andy said, staring at me to see what I thought of the stranger's offer.

"Okay, fine," I said, after a few moments, taking one more quick look at Ahmet.

We obviously needed help figuring out where to go in this mass of humanity and traffic. Ahmet seemed legitimate enough. We had no planned itinerary for taking in the sights, nor any idea about local transportation other than the city bus. We shook hands with him once more as if to seal the deal.

Off we went, the three of us, down the street to Ahmet's car. Gulu, his muscular but friendly, 20-something, non English-speaking driver, sat behind the wheel.

Andy and I huddled together in the tiny backseat, knees pressed against the back of the front seat. Ahmet sat on the passenger side scanning a map. Gulu confidently commandeered our compact car through a maze of other European-sized cars. His skill weaving briskly from lane to lane on a busy, six-lane boulevard in the heart of the city was impressive. Ahmet popped a cassette of Turkish music into his tape player and reached back holding a small bottle of liquid that looked like water.

"Hold out your hands," Ahmet said as he gave each of our outstretched palms a squirt. "It's tradition. Lemon cologne. Turkish refreshment. Rub your hands together; then rub your face. You'll feel better."

By the end of our first day in Istanbul, thanks to Ahmet and Gulu, we had toured the old city by car, then on foot at strategic tourist spots. We had our picture taken in front of the ancient Roman Hippodrome, the 3,500-year-old obelisk brought from Egypt in 390, C.E., visited the Museum of Turkish and Islamic Arts where we enjoyed a light lunch, the Galata Tower, the Kariye Museum filled with stunning Christian frescos, and the Blue Mosque (our first visit inside a mosque; in Saudi Arabia they are off-limits to non-Muslims).

Ahmet mentioned to Andy he was co-owner of a well-established carpet shop with a wide selection of hand-woven carpets. By late afternoon, we ended up at Ahmet's shop where he guided us to two comfortable, overstuffed chairs and told us to relax while he ordered tea. Ahmet was a master at making us feel special, and we loved it. Buying a carpet in the Middle East is an involved process and one that takes time, tea, manipulation, haggling, intuition and more tea. Andy had studied up on

Oriental rugs and was better at negotiating than I, so I let him ask all the questions, although he did consult me before making our final purchases. Ahmet wanted payment in American dollars since Turkish lira was losing value and the American dollar was stable.

An hour and a half later, we had bought a wool nomad carpet and a silk Hereke carpet. Andy also bought a tan suede jacket lined in sheep's wool from Ahmet's shop. After adding up our expenditures, we realized we had spent our budgeted amount for discretionary spending, all on the first day. We promised each other no more rugs, no more coats, no more anything we would have to carry home with us.

As we gathered up our purchases and prepared to return to our hotel, Ahmet said he knew of a traditional Turkish tavern, Alex's, serving authentic Turkish food and drinks.

"Live Turkish music for dancing . . . and belly dancers," he added, looking at Andy with a twinkle in his eye.

Ahmet told us his girlfriend Susan was visiting from London and suggested all five of us go together. Andy and I agreed it sounded like fun and told Ahmet we'd join them. When Andy asked Ahmet what he owed him for the tour that day, Ahmet brushed him away.

"Nothing, my brother for life, nothing," he said.

In a gesture of appreciation, Andy offered to pay for dinner. Ahmet volunteered to make dinner reservations. Gulu dropped us off at our hotel to freshen up and said he'd pick us up at 7:30. When the three of them pulled in front of our hotel, I was impressed that Susan got out of the car to shake hands and greet us. She was American, an attractive, blue-eyed, blond living and working in London, friendly and easy to talk with. We didn't ask questions about their relationship and they never told us how they met. She, Andy and I sat shoulder-to-shoulder in the backseat.

When we walked into Alex's that evening, the place was alive with music and laughter. Band members played with gusto—bass, drums, acoustic bass guitar, piccolo and accordion. Couples danced on the generous-sized dance floor with skirts twirling, onlookers clapping. A male vocalist warbled away keeping up with the beat of the band. If Ahmet hadn't made reservations, we never would have had such a ringside seat. Ours was the last empty table close to the dance floor. Ahmet ordered a Turkish meal for us to share: wrapped vine leaves filled with rice, onion and spices that tasted like mint, currant, pepper and cinnamon; fried eggplant with onion, parsley, garlic and a tasty tomato sauce; lamb, beef and chicken kebabs on a skewer and grilled to perfection over a charcoal fire; a refreshing mixture of sliced cucumbers with yogurt, garlic and mint. He, Susan and Andy had wine and a glass of ouzo, an anise-flavored alcoholic drink, popular in Turkey. Gulu and I passed on the alcohol, sticking to iced tea instead. Afterward, we enjoyed coffee and a typical Turkish dessert of caramelized carrots with cinnamon, walnuts, hazelnuts and pistachios all covered with grated coconut, rice pudding and a popular sweet confection called Turkish delight.

Andy pushed back his chair and held out his hand.

"Time to dance," he said, pulling me up and onto the dance floor.

It felt good to be held in my husband's firm embrace in public as we mostly kept up with the unfamiliar beat of the band while trying not to step on each other's toes. I couldn't remember the last time we had danced together to a live band. How mistaken I was about Turkey not being a romantic honeymoon destination. Caught up in the moment—I felt relaxed and carefree. I was a new bride, deeply in love with my husband, celebrating life and love with people we've never seen before and doubted if we would ever see again. This unanticipated, improbable, somewhat outrageous and yet unforgettable evening was topped off by an exotic looking, well endowed, bleached-blond belly dancer appearing out of nowhere, stepping gracefully up and onto our table, seductively twirling her hips to the music as we all clapped and stared. Andy appeared embarrassed as he tucked a bill or two into the top of her low-hung bikini skirt of sequined streamers to show our appreciation.

On our way back to the hotel, Ahmet, who kept referring to us as "my brother and sister for life" invited us to go along the next day to Yalova for the weekend. He, Susan and Gulu were taking a few days off to stay at a resort lodge in the Termal district of Turkey, famous for its hot-springs baths. Gulu would drive Ahmet's car. Once more, we're faced with a decision. We agreed it sounded intriguing and told Ahmet we'd go for one night. Ahmet offered to call the lodge to reserve our room and said they'd pick us up next morning at 9:00. They would stay until Monday but Gulu would drive us to the ferry Sunday morning after breakfast so we could return to Istanbul on our own.

Gulu crammed our two small bags next to theirs into the trunk of his car, and we were off. Once again, Ahmet and Gulu sat in the front seat and Susan, Andy and I sat shoulder-to-shoulder in the backseat. We crossed a bridge over the Bosphorus River, from the western or European side of Turkey, to the eastern, or Asian side, and drove several hours to the Sea of Marmara. There, we boarded a ferryboat for a 45-minute ride to the southern coast. From there, our lodge was another 45-minute drive into the mountains.

Set in lush and dream-like surroundings of hilly terrain, resplendent with assorted greenery and wild flowers, poppies, and baby's breath, our lodge was, in fact, a modern hotel. We told Ahmet, Susan and Gulu we'd meet them for dinner in the dining room at 7:30. After settling into our rustic but clean and comfortable room, we headed for the hot springs baths, located a quarter-mile through heavy vegetation on a boardwalk from the lodge.

Once inside the entrance, Andy paid the clerk who handed us bathing suits, wooden clog shoes and Turkish towels. We entered dressing rooms through separate areas, one for 'males' the other for 'females'. The bath area, a huge, dimly lit open space similar to Roman catacombs, with low stone ceilings, stone walls and marble floors, contained four large pools of steaming hot water. The room was eerily quiet other than a hissing sound like steam being released from a pressure cooker. The cool air accounted for the hot steam fogging up my glasses. I couldn't recognize Andy amongst all the human forms milling around the decks and in the pools. Fortunately, he found me first and together we laid our robes on an empty deck chair and slid into the just-right, medium-hot water of the first soaking pool. The water was three to four feet deep, with ledges around the sides of the pools for sitting. Silent human forms standing in the pool and resting along the sides appeared as out-of-focus shapes. I couldn't tell if they were male or female so there was no greeting each other, waving or socializing. We moved from there to the larger pool, this one heated to 185° Fahrenheit, again, filled with other bathers. Although we never submerged our heads under water, we were dripping with sweat.

About twenty minutes later, we had had enough. We emerged from the pool, put on our robes and walked to a rest area with deck chairs. A kindly older woman in a white uniform served us huge glasses of ice-cold apple juice with sugar cubes and a slice of fresh lemon. After enjoying our welcome refreshment, we dressed, walked back to our room on rubbery legs and collapsed on the bed. Our energy depleted from the steam bath, we nearly overslept, yet awoke in time to shower and dress for dinner.

Next morning at breakfast, Andy asked Ahmet what we owed him for his services. "Nothing, my brother for life; nothing," he said.

We could hardly believe his generosity but we *had* purchased two carpets and a coat at his shop and paid for everyone's dinner at Alex's. If Ahmet felt it was fair, it was fair. We thanked him once again, said our good-byes and left. Gulu drove us back to the ferry dock.

Just as the ferry arrived to carry us across the Sea of Marmara, it began to rain. We fell in line behind increasing numbers of silent and somber passengers eager to get inside the ferry. The main passenger area was filled with rows of wooden benches. We found two seats on a bench near a window. A steady stream of humble looking passengers of all ages came aboard. There were ladies wearing babushkas and carrying bags. The men all had bushy eyebrows and mustaches; some walked with canes. Even the children appeared solemn, as if accustomed to waiting their turn. This wasn't a pleasure trip packed with happy tourists. These were local folks, living through difficult times with equanimity.

About 45 minutes into our ride, a tall, thin, slightly stooped man with graying hair stood off to the side near the middle isle. He had deep wrinkles under his eyes, and his face and neck hadn't been shaved for a while. He wore baggy pants, a threadbare blazer, and a black cap on his head. Showing no emotion, he began speaking in a loud monotone to nobody in particular, in what we assumed was Turkish. Several of his front teeth were missing. From one of three plastic bags at his feet he brought out a wide, white elastic band. With large, muscular hands, he began pulling the garment in and out, in and out to demonstrate its easy flexibility.

"Girdle," I whispered to Andy who nodded.

Nobody in this crowd appeared interested. A new girdle was an extravagance few Turkish people could afford. Besides, who would have the courage to purchase something so personal in a roomful of staring witnesses? With no customers coming forward, the man folded up the garment, put it in a plastic bag and took out a much larger garment. This one was a soft, pinkish tan in color. Same as before, he stretched it in and out a few times, turning right and left, showing it around the room. Once again, no takers.

He folded up the larger girdle, stuffed it in a plastic bag and pulled out a child's toy—two colorful plastic birds with flapping wings, each tied to a wooden stick. As the man twirled the stick, the birds flew around in circles. A young boy came up with his little sister beside him. The boy wore a cap; the girl wore a scarf. The boy handed the man money to buy the birds. Both children appeared expressionless as they returned to their mother who watched solemnly from several rows away. The salesman gathered up his bags and headed toward another area of the ferry.

Once back in Istanbul, we caught a bus to our hotel and dropped off our bags. In the afternoon, we toured St. Sophia, also known as Hagia Sophia, considered the world's supreme masterpiece of Byzantine art. We also visited the opulent Dolmabahce Palace, home of the world's largest chandelier, weighing four-and-a-half tons, and where nearly two-thirds of the palace had once been occupied by harem females. We noticed that all the clocks in the palace were stopped at 9:05. Our guide said this was in memory of President Kemal Ataturk—Turkey's first president in 1923, who implemented reforms that rapidly secularized and westernized the country. He died at the palace on November 10, 1938—precisely at 9:05 a.m.

The next day, we planned to fly to Izmir, located in the southeastern part of Turkey on the Mediterranean coast. Izmir was the closest airport to Kusadasi, our final destination, farther down the coast of the Mediterranean Sea. Andy's hospital friends told him Kusadasi was a popular vacation spot. Our 'brother for life' Ahmet, had a cousin, Ajlan, who owned a hotel in Kusadasi so he kindly made arrangements for us to stay there.

After a two-hour plane ride the next day from Istanbul to Izmir, we caught a bus to Kusadasi, arriving well after dark. Everyone on the bus smoked—everyone except us. It rained all the way, so every window on the bus was closed. The bus dropped us off near what appeared to be the center of town, under a streetlight. As I watched the bus disappear down the road, I felt like crying. I didn't want to complain and detract from the good time we had in Istanbul, but I wasn't pleased about taking the bus rather than rent a car of our own. We stood in the rain without umbrellas, in the dark, smelling like cigarettes, holding our suitcases, not knowing how to get to our hotel. As much as I wanted to, I didn't say a word. I was afraid if I opened my mouth, I'd say something I'd later regret. How we found our way without only a few streetlights to guide us felt like a miracle. I simply followed Andy, who soon spotted Ahmet's cousin's hotel on a side street. We walked in the front door and saw four men playing cards around a table in the lobby, under a thick cloud of cigarette smoke. Immersed in their game, they didn't see us standing there. Turkish music with its distinctive mix of undulating tribal drumming played in the background.

"Hello," Andy called out. The man closest to the door stood up, and came toward us with his hand extended.

"Welcome, my friend. My name is Ajlan."

"Ajlan," Andy said taking his hand, "your cousin Ahmet said you have a room for us. I'm Andy. This is Pam." I managed a faint smile.

Once he realized we were Ahmet's friends, Ajlan couldn't have been more gracious. He was in his mid- 30s, dark hair and dark eyes, a slight beard, and wore a dark shirt and blue jeans. His English wasn't as good as Andy's Arabic. He led us upstairs, unlocked the door at the top of the stairs and motioned for us to enter.

"This our best room in the house," he said. "Number one room for you—number-one guests."

I glanced around the sparsely furnished room and peeked inside the tiny bathroom. This place made our hotel in Istanbul seem luxurious. When we asked about a local restaurant, Ajlan pointed toward town.

By the time we changed out of our wet clothes, put on sweaters, rain parkas and got out onto the sidewalk, the rain had stopped. We walked two blocks to the main street and found a pizza shop that sold bottled wine. The pizza was inedible so we gave it to two feral cats meowing at the door. The wine was okay, so Andy corked the bottle and brought it with us. On our way back to our hotel, we saw a light on in a small bakery and stopped to buy a loaf of bread. We went back to our room and had bread and wine for dinner.

"Why don't you take a hot bath before turning in?" Andy suggested, hoping a 'tubby' would lighten my mood. "You'll feel better."

When I turned on the bathtub faucet, the water was ice cold, even after I let it run a while. Andy went down to speak with Ajlan who told him a hot bath or shower before bed depended on sunshine that day. Water was heated in holding tanks on rooftops. No sunshine during the day, no hot water at night. In Riyadh, our water was heated in the same way, but we had sunshine every day. In Turkey, sunshine was unpredictable. I was desperate for something, anything to make me feel better.

"I'm calling Mother," I said, glancing at my watch. "It's almost 10 here; it's the middle of the afternoon in Ohio. I presume Ajlan has a functional phone somewhere?"

Ajlan was standing behind the counter when Andy and I came downstairs.

"My wife wishes to make a phone call. Is there a phone she can use?"

"No problem," Ajlan said, looking at me with raised eyebrows I took to be a sign of wanting to please.

We followed him through a door and down a dark, narrow hallway with a low ceiling into a closet lined with shelves. He switched on the light—an overhead light bulb dangling at the end of an electric cord—and reached behind some boxes on one of the middle shelves. He pulled out a black, old-fashioned, dial telephone, the likes of which I hadn't seen for 30 years.

"Where you calling?" he said as he handed me the phone.

"Worthington, a town in Ohio, in the United States."

His eyes opened wide as he looked at Andy with shocked disbelief. Speaking directly to Andy, he said "Expensive, very expensive." Turning to me he said, "Don't talk long."

"We'll pay whatever it costs," I said looking him in the eye. "It's her eighty-second birthday and I'm calling her."

I took the receiver from his hand and gave it to Andy. I held the phone and dialed the number. My heart sank as Mother's phone rang four times, then five.

"Pammy, how wonderful to hear from you," Mother said when she finally picked up.

Two days earlier was her actual birthday, but I didn't have access to a phone so this was her birthday call. Mother was born and raised on a small farm in rural Ohio and lived in Ohio all her life. She worked at a daily newspaper in Columbus for fourteen years before she and Daddy were married. She always had a keen interest in world affairs and different cultures, so she seemed genuinely excited for Andy and me to be honeymooning in Turkey. Her enthusiasm over the phone lifted my spirits. Instead of seeking sympathy by going down my long list of complaints and frustrations such as a long bus ride, cold and drizzling rain, inedible pizza, no hot water, I found myself telling her how interesting Turkey was—how exotic, how charming, how educational. I envisioned her writing down everything I said so she could tell my sisters and aunts about where Andy and

I were staying and what we were doing in Turkey.

A few minutes into the call, Ajlan began fidgeting, shaking his head and shifting from foot to foot. I was already annoyed to have him crammed in this diminutive closet with Andy and me. He began making hand gestures to Andy suggesting I hang up. Ignoring him, I turned my back and continued talking. When I overheard Andy whispering to Ajlan that I would only talk a few more minutes, I decided I'd better say goodbye to Mother and ring off.

"How much do we owe you?" Andy asked.

"She talk seven minutes at 6,000 lira per minute, that's 42,000 lira," said Ajlan.

Andy gave him 50,000 lira ($25) and shook his hand.

"Thank you, thank you," Ajlan said as he bowed to both of us.

I was touched that Ajlan accepted the money with such gratitude, as if he had won the lottery. He returned the phone to its hiding place behind the boxes on the shelf. Andy and I said goodnight, found our way back to the stairs and up to our room.

Although I hadn't read *The Ugly American*, published some years earlier, I was aware of the impression some Americans had made by expecting and demanding the same quality and service overseas that are available in the U.S. The book describes American fictional characters whose arrogance and failure to understand local culture created bad feelings around the world. Was I being *that* kind of ugly American?

Reflecting on the day that started out with eager anticipation and ended with so many frustrations and disappointments, I paused when I thought about what we had eaten for dinner. What at first seemed like a bad joke on us became an unexpected blessing. We ate bread and drank wine for our dinner—the Sacraments of the Eucharist. In my preoccupation with what went wrong, I forgot to think about what went right. God Himself had tapped me on the shoulder as if to say, "Aren't you missing something, Pam?"

Feeling contrite and embarrassed, I turned to Andy.

"I'm beginning to feel guilty for the way I spoke to Ahmet's cousin," I said. "I think I'm spoiled by the good life I've grown accustomed to back home, while forgetting more than half the world lives in what we consider poverty. Seeing how resourceful and resilient yet cheerful the Turkish people are with so few material comforts makes me contrite. It's not what I expected in the way of a honeymoon, but perhaps there's a lesson for me in Turkey. I'm thinking it's humility."

The next morning, we awoke to blue sky and sunshine outside the open window of our room—definitely an improvement over yesterday's weather. Not more than 50 yards away, we watched a young boy riding a donkey up a rocky and barren dirt hill next to our hotel. With one hand the boy was gripping the donkey's reins. With the other he was gripping loaves of bread.

"There goes our breakfast," I said, half jokingly.

A short while later we saw the same boy putting out large trays of sliced bread on the serving table in the dining room downstairs. For breakfast that morning, along with hot Turkish coffee and freshly baked bread, we enjoyed sun-ripened, sliced tomatoes, apricot jam, hard-boiled eggs, olives, and sliced cheese—all locally grown and homemade. After last night's disappointing pizza, we relished such a delicious breakfast in humble yet clean surroundings.

With our stomachs full and the entire day ahead of us, we asked Ahmet's cousin for sightseeing suggestions. He told us we could take a bus to Selcuk, a small village not far away, where we would be close enough to Ephesus and Mary's House to take a cab.

"Mary's House?" I said. "What's that?"

"Special place," he said reverently. "Very special."

We had never heard of Mary's House and Ajlan didn't have a good enough command of English to explain what made it so special. We simply followed his directions to the bus station and purchased two tickets to Selcuk, seven miles away. We rode through open countryside, gently rolling hills covered with rows and rows of olive trees dotting the landscape. We saw men, women and children working in the fields, bent over in the early morning sun, picking cotton. Our bus occasionally passed what appeared to be three-generation families, grandparents, parents and children walking along the side of the road, some without shoes, and an occasional horse-drawn cart carrying baskets of potatoes, tomatoes, squash and other fall crops. The countryside in Turkey had no four- or six-lane highways, no billboards, no traffic lights, no heavy traffic, no roadside rest stops or gasoline stations like back home.

Selcuk was a small village with only a café, a gas station and a grocery store. We asked at the gas station about Mary's House and Ephesus. A man working there told us we could catch a cab down at the corner that would take us to the top of Nightingale Mountain and Mary's House.

Our cab driver nodded when Andy told him where we wanted to go. Andy paid him for a one-way ride to the top of the mountain since we assumed we could later get a cab back down to Ephesus. The cab, well worn inside and out, wasn't equipped with seat belts. The narrow gravel road twisted and turned up the mountain, lined on either side with trees and dense foliage. Our driver had a heavy foot and didn't speak much English. I hesitated to tell him to slow down because I didn't want to distract him. We never passed a car coming down the mountain, thank goodness, and made it safely to the top. The driver let us out at the end of the road. We thanked him and began walking up a stone-covered path toward Mary's House. The path was lined on either side with mature olive trees. Ahead, we could see a tiny stone cottage at a distance, tucked into the side of the mountain. We saw no crowds of tourists, only a few people standing on the grass in front of the cottage, and no commercial establishments or food stands selling drinks, snacks or souvenirs. We paused to read a large sign written in English, German and French, posted along the walkway.

Notice About the Shrine

This place is considered to be the last home of the Blessed Virgin, the Mother of Jesus Christ. St. John, in his gospel, tells us that Jesus, before dying on the cross, entrusted to him the care of his Mother when he said: "Behold thy mother." And from that hour Saint John took her to his own. The "Acts of the Apostles" relate how after the death of Christ, his followers were persecuted in Jerusalem. St. Stephen was stoned in 37 A.D. St. James was beheaded in 42 A.D. And they further relate how they divided the world between them for preaching the Gospel, and St. John was given Asia Minor. Now, Mary had been given to his care, and with the persecutions, probably brought her with him to Asia Minor.

The Facts are Confirmed Historically

There are two evidences—(1) The presence of the tomb of St. John in Ephesus; and (2) The presence of the first Basilica of the world dedicated to the Blessed Virgin. In the early days of the church, places of worship were only dedicated to persons who had lived or died in the locality. Also, the Ecumenical Council of 431 was held in Ephesus in this Basilica for the definition of the dogma of the Divine Motherhood of Mary. The Council Fathers write about Nestorius, "... after his arrival to Ephesus where John the Theologian and the Holy Virgin Mary, Mother of God... " There is another confirmation in the oral tradition of the villagers of Kirkindje. These people were the descendants of the Christians of Ephesus. They had passed from generation to generation the belief of the death of Mary in this place that they called PANAGHIA KAPULU. They have kept this tradition alive through the annual pilgrimage of 15th August.

Discovery of This Place in 19th Century

During the 19th century, the book "Life of the Blessed Virgin" was published in Germany. The material for this book come [sic] from the revelations of a stigmatized nun, Anna Catherina Emmerich. She was an invalid that never left Germany. In her visions, she described with amazing accuracy the hills of Ephesus and the house where she saw the Blessed Virgin spending her last years. Accordingly, two scientific expeditions were organized and they found this place perfectly agreeing with her descriptions.

The Chapel

The chapel was rebuilt upon the original foundations that have been determined to date as of the 1st and 4th centuries. Part of the re-building is of the 7th century and the last restoration took place in 1951.

With new knowledge of where we were, we reverently entered the first room of the cottage, a relatively small vestibule with ledges on either side filled with sand and lighted, flickering candles. Sunlight streamed through closed windows on the east side of the structure. A small group of German tourists, all dressed in hiking clothes, stood to one side of the room, hats in hands, quietly singing *Silent Night*, in German. A container filled with candles caught my eye. We paid for six candles: one to light for our children and families, and five to take with us, one for each of our four children and one for us.

Beyond the vestibule, we entered the main area of the chapel, with a high window on either side of the room. We stood in silence, taking in the simple beauty and sacredness of this place where Mary the Mother of Christ spent her last days of life on Earth. I was awestruck to be in such a sacred place. I imagined what it was like 2,000 years before when she was actually there, living and breathing where Andy and I were now standing. I thanked God for giving us the opportunity to be there together. I prayed for all our children, our parents, our siblings, other family members and friends. As we left that day and rode back down Nightingale Mountain, I reflected on my initial hesitation when Andy first mentioned Turkey for our honeymoon. What began that day as a spontaneous excursion turned out to be a memorable experience.

Later that day, we visited Ephesus, considered the world's best-preserved classical city, dating to at least 1300 B.C. At one time Asia Minor's largest metropolis and principal port, it was now a huge area covered as far as the eye could see with marble ruins, some partially restored, many in disarray. We walked among them trying to imagine St. Paul preaching there to small groups of Jews and Gentiles centuries before. The Turkish people, struggling for financial stability, had this enormous treasure trove of ancient ruins to preserve and protect for perpetuity; yet we saw no signs explaining where we were or what had been there in the time of Jesus and for centuries after his crucifixion and resurrection.

We later learned that not far from Mary's House, Mary Magdalene's remains were discovered in a sarcophagus unearthed in 1952, and positively identified by Professor Louis Massignon of the College de France[14]. Also in Ephesus, we discovered the tomb of St. John, an unmarked tomb at the bottom of a gated stairway, out in the middle of an expansive marble plateau with other ruins scattered all around. We were the only tourists that day.

Once again, I felt the thrill and power of 'place,' of physically being where an extraordinary individual once stood or something remarkable and historically significant happened. In Turkey, we were closer to where Jesus was born, lived and died, than we were in Riyadh. Even though I had attended church regularly after my divorce, I still had many questions about

---

[14] *Mary's House ~ The Extraordinary Story Behind the Discovery of the House Where the Virgin Mary Lived and Died*, by David Carroll, Christian Classics ©2002

the meaning of life, death, suffering, forgiveness and love. Now, as a new Catholic, I still had much to learn about the Catholic faith and about Christianity in general. I wondered why, if one God created our Universe, all religions continued to be at odds with each other. I told Andy whatever else we saw or did in the remaining eight days of our honeymoon could not compare with our visit to Mary's House.

Yet, there was still much to see and do in Turkey. The next day, we took a bus ride south along the coast to Bodrum, a quaint seaport, and spent the day exploring the small village and surrounding hillside. Unfortunately, we had to cancel a boat trip to Samos, a Greek island nearby, because of rain. The day we left Kusadasi the sky was clear and sunny. Our bus ride this time was more pleasant—all the windows on the bus were open and only a few smokers on board. We went directly to the Izmir airport for a return flight to Istanbul, eager to see the sights we hadn't seen before.

Our hotel, Otel Pamphylia, set in Instanbul's historic Sultanahmet district, looked more like the tower of a medieval castle than a hotel. All seven floors were accessible by circular stairs on the outside next to the walls with a diminutive elevator in the middle of the tower. Our modest room was on floor seven. The hotel's café was in the basement where every day we enjoyed a typical Turkish breakfast—bread, hardboiled eggs, cheese, tomatoes, olives, and coffee.

On Sunday morning, we attended Mass at the Greek Orthodox Church near Taksim Square in the modern section of Istanbul. We entered the ancient church with reverence, as it had been our first time to worship together since our wedding in June. After my Protestant upbringing, I wondered at times if I would ever feel or be completely Catholic. I trusted God to accept me as I was, without labels. I felt His presence in that ancient and spacious sanctuary as natural sunlight streamed through stained glass windows lighting up every recess and corner. An organ played softly as mostly older worshipers filed into the pews, heads bowed.

Mass was delivered in Turkish so we followed the liturgy on memory alone as we listened to the homily, the prayers and singing with open hearts and minds. We both offered prayers for our children, parents, families and friends back home, asking God to keep them healthy and happy. When it came time for the Eucharist, we were surprised when the bread and wine were passed in trays, similar to how communion was served in my Presbyterian Church back home. As soon as the Eucharist was over, so was the service—the suddenness of it was remarkable. No prayers, no hymns, no announcements. Just like that—it was over and done. People stood up, walked slowly from their pews, faced the front of the sanctuary, made the sign of the cross, bowed toward the altar and walked out of the sanctuary.

We spent several hours walking through the magnificent Grand Bazaar, built in 1461, with thousands of vendors selling exotic wares from carpets to jewelry to spices and antiques. We also toured the opulent Topkapi Palace, the primary residence of the Ottoman Sultans from 1465 to 1856. We strolled across the Galata Bridge, built over the Golden Horn in the 6th century by Julian the Great, now crowded with shops and restaurants, and later took a boat ride down the Bosphorus River to the Black Sea.

On the morning of our departure, as I was waking up, Andy whispered in my ear, "Good news, bad news."

"Good news," I mumbled.

"You don't have to take a cold shower this morning."

"Great," I said, opening one eye. "What's the bad news?"

"There's no water."

This wasn't the only problem that day. The elevator wasn't functional. We walked down seven flights of stairs to the breakfast room in the cellar, packed with other guests looking as disheveled as we did, all eating in silence. After breakfast, we climbed the stairs to our room. With only two small suitcases, we had to pack both rugs *and* Andy's new leather coat since he already had a coat to wear home. The clothes that wouldn't fit into either suitcase—my skirt, three blouses and an extra sweater—became part of my travel outfit. I had to roll up the legs of my long pants underneath my skirt, which added more than a few inches to my hips. I put on three blouses, tightest one first (two of them were long-sleeved), my long-sleeved turtleneck sweater and a heavier cardigan sweater—all crammed underneath my raincoat. My arms looked like sausages.

    To make matters worse, neither of us had showered, Andy hadn't shaved, and we couldn't wash our faces or brush our teeth. I was certain we wouldn't see anyone we knew at the airport in Istanbul, but I worried about landing in Riyadh. Besides humility and gratitude, our honeymoon in Turkey taught me to have a sense of humor, to trust my instincts, and expect the unexpected while traveling. All were important life lessons I would have to relearn many times over, once back in Riyadh.

Chapter 6

New Opportunity

Our plane touched down at 1:30 Friday morning and not a moment too soon. I was desperate for a hot shower and sleep. In spite of my best intentions hours earlier to remain humble and grateful, my mood had deteriorated. It wasn't so much that I was bone tired, hadn't bathed in two days and was wearing a week's worth of dirty laundry. I was depressed because coming home to Riyadh didn't feel like coming home, the kind of coming home feeling you get when you've been away and can't wait to call your family to make sure they're okay and let them know you're okay, too. We had none of that welcome-home feeling in that hot, dark, early morning hour. The reality of this stark-looking villa *being our home* was discouraging.

We went to bed without unpacking and slept until noon on Friday. We had all day to unpack, do laundry, go out to buy a few groceries, and try calling our families. We couldn't reach any of the kids but were grateful to speak briefly with Andy's parents and my mother. Everyone seemed healthy and happy in spite of our absence. It was back to work the next day.

When I walked into the office Saturday morning, Suhair greeted me with a warm smile.

"We missed you, Pam," she said. "They need you here more than they're willing to admit."

Nabiha sat at her desk, waiting for someone on the other end of the phone. She looked up from her desk and waved.

"Welcome back, Pam," she whispered. "Mr. Al Senaidy wants to see you in his office. *Right away*."

"How's your husband?" he said as I walked in the door, motioning for me to sit in the chair next to his desk.

"Fine, fine," I answered. "He'll be pleased to know you asked about him."

"How was your holiday?"

"Wonderful," I said. "We loved it."

"Good, good," he said. "Help yourself to dates."

By now I had come to appreciate Mr. Al Senaidy's sunny disposition—and felt amused rather than bewildered when he, and all other male Saudis I knew at the hospital, greeted me by first asking about my husband.

"No, thank you," I said. "I just ate breakfast. Maybe later."

He handed me a copy of his outline for the November *Bulletin*. I was surprised his list didn't include the hospital's seventh anniversary coming up on November 29th.

"What do you think about an article highlighting the hospital's growth and progress since opening day?" I said. "After all, King Fahad is now a 500-bed tertiary hospital approved by the Joint Commission on the Accreditation of Health Care Organizations. Perhaps we could get a photo of current employees who were here opening day and interview them."

"Yes, yes," Mr. Al Senaidy said, pausing to consider my suggestion. "Will you write the article and arrange for the photo?"

"Yes, of course," I said. "I'll work with Nabiha and Suhair and perhaps even interview Bill Towle and Dr. Al-Sharidah.

"Great," he said.

My self-imposed assignment had more responsibility and creative potential than I had previously been given. Conducting interviews with physicians, nurses and technicians about why they chose to work in Saudi Arabia appealed to me. I had covered enough assignments about Islam and Islamic culture, historic cities in The Kingdom and informational stories about common winter diseases.

About this time, I rode back to our villa on the shuttle bus with my neighbor, Sue Godfry. Sue was grocery shopping at Medical City and I was coming home from work. She and I had only seen each other in passing but never stopped to chat. Her husband, Chris, was a trauma physician so he and Andy knew each other from the hospital. Sue was in her early 30s with young children so we didn't have much in common. The day after I saw her on the bus, she telephoned to invite me over for coffee. I called Nabiha and told her I'd be late since it was a work day for me.

"What exactly do you do for Public Affairs?" Sue asked as she poured two cups of freshly brewed coffee.

"Good question," I said. "I'm never sure what is expected of me. My formal job description doesn't match what I actually do day to day. Like everyone else who works there, I have good days and bad days. Right now, bad days are outnumbering the good days. My claim to fame is I'm the first Christian, female, Westerner to work as a writer in the Public Affairs Department. My challenge is that all my bosses are Saudi males. Abdullah keeps trying to convert me to Islam. He promised to slaughter a lamb and celebrate with a desert cookout when I do. No chance of that happening anytime soon."

I helped myself to one of Sue's melt-in-your-mouth homemade

chocolate chip cookies as she began to tell me about her interests, her background, what brought them to Saudi Arabia, and their families. She and Chris were Canadians who loved traveling with their kids. Physicians received generous paid-vacation time, so the Godfreys took advantage of being close to Asia, Africa and other parts of the Middle East. Sue showed me photographs of some of their travels. I couldn't help but wish Andy and I were able to do the same with our children; but, of course, they were older and our situation was different. My visit with Sue flew by. Soon, it was time to head back to the hospital.

"You know, Pam, there's someone you must meet," she said, almost as an afterthought. "She's a writer, here in Riyadh. Her name is Kathy Cuddihy. She and her husband Sean have lived here for 13 years. Kathy's Canadian; Sean's Irish. He's an engineer for Bechtel."

"I'd love to meet her," I said, with a rush of excitement.

"I'll see if I can arrange a dinner with the six of us."

Sue called later to ask if we were free on Sunday.

"Do you and Andy like Indian?" she asked.

"Love it," I said.

"Be ready at 6:30. We'll drive."

Cuddihys pulled into the parking lot of Godfeys' favorite Indian restaurant seconds after we arrived. Once introductions were made, I knew it would be a fun evening. Kathy seemed as excited to meet me as I was to meet her. We sat next to each other at the table and never ran out of things to talk about. She, too, was a devoted wife and mother who reluctantly agreed to come to Riyadh 14 years earlier because of Sean's new job. She had an engaging sense of humor and a positive attitude toward cultural restrictions imposed on Western females. While Kathy respected and appreciated reasonable Saudi customs and culture, she ignored the more restrictive rules for non-Muslim females. She refused to wear an abaya when dressed modestly, or to refrain from speaking out in mixed company. Kathy had what I lacked as a newcomer to the Kingdom—boldness and confidence, connections and experience. As a well-known writer in Saudi Arabia, Kathy was a seasoned professional when mingling with well-traveled men and women from different countries. She loved telling me about her connections and adventures and I loved hearing them. She was the first Western female I had encountered who seemed actually excited about living here.

When we said good-bye at the restaurant, Kathy told me she'd call in a day or two to arrange for us to meet at her place to discuss some free-lance writing opportunities for me. As soon as Godfreys dropped us off in front of our villa, I somewhat timidly asked Andy for a favor.

"Did you hear Kathy say she would invite me to their villa next week?"

"No, but that's great," he said. "You're going aren't you?"

"Well . . . yes, but I'm nervous about going off compound by myself. Could you *please* take a few hours off that day to drive me to Al Yamama compound? I'm sure you could wait inside while we talked, read a book or magazine. I plan to stay only a couple of hours. I'll bet Kathy would offer you a glass of Sean's homemade wine he was telling you about at dinner."

Andy gave me a look of disbelief. "You've got to be kidding."

"The limo drivers here terrify me," I continued, ignoring his skepticism. "They drive too fast and I've never known any of them to speak English. Besides, I don't know how to arrange for a limo."

Taxis in Riyadh were called limousines or 'limos' for short. For me, raised in the 1950s, the word 'limo' conjured up images of a shiny black or white, six- or eight-door Cadillac for movie stars. Most 'limos' in Riyadh were four-door vehicles that looked like demolition derby survivors.

"It's easy," Andy said. "All you do is call the limo service at MC and ask for an English-speaking driver. Chances are you'll get a Filipino, Yemeni or Bangladeshi who knows rudimentary English. They'll take you anywhere you want."

"Is it safe?"

"Of course it's safe. Do you think I'd tell you to go if it wasn't?"

Kathy and I made a date for the following week. I phoned MC limo service and asked an English-speaking driver. The fellow who appeared at our villa did not speak English.

"Al Ya-ma-ma Com-pound," I said loudly and slowly, pronouncing each syllable. The driver gave me a puzzled look. I handed him the map Andy drew by hand. He studied it carefully and then broke into a toothless grin.

"Aiwa. Mafee mushkala. Inshallah[15]," he said.

Grateful for his response that I could understand, I settled back and off we went across the desert. When we arrived at the Al Yamama gate, the guard checked my identification papers and waved us in. My limo driver turned down Kathy's street and dropped me off on time, safe and sound. I chided myself for all that worrying for nothing.

Kathy and Sean's villa was larger and more inviting, more comfortable, more Western than ours; plus, their villa was beautifully landscaped with cactus plants and flowering vines and shrubbery. During their 13 years in Saudi Arabia, the Cuddihys had accumulated numerous

---

[15] Yes. No problem. God willing.

artifacts and pieces of fine art, antiques and other treasures, all with fascinating stories.

Unlike King Fahad National Guard Compound where all expats living there worked at the hospital, Al Yamama was home to expats of many nationalities working in Riyadh at an executive or professional level for a variety of businesses and corporations.

Kathy met me at the front door with the Saudi/European, two-cheek, air-kiss, big-smile, warm-hug greeting. She gave me a quick tour of their villa where they lived with their daughter, Tara, 13, and son, Kieran, 11. Seeing evidence of children in their home—tennis shoes and rackets, ball and bat, bicycles and roller skates lined up neatly by the back door—gave their villa that homey, family feeling ours lacked.

Kathy invited me to pull up a chair as she placed a pot of hot tea and a plate of petite sandwiches and homemade cookies on the table. While I loved the informality of our surroundings, I also appreciated the civilized refinements she set out—a small vase of fresh flowers, cloth napkins, sugar cubes, honey and fresh lemon slices.

"So," I said, after Kathy filled our cups with the fragrant tea, "tell me about your writing here in Riyadh."

"I've just published a book about my experiences as a Saudi expat, and I'm working on another about motherhood," she said. "I also have a weekly column, *Kathy's Korner*, in the *Saudi Gazette* that keeps me fairly busy. I also do part-time, free-lance writing and public relations for the King Faisal Foundation. That's where you might come in after the first of the year, if you're interested."

"I'm interested alright," I said. "Tell me more."

What I felt like saying was I hadn't written for an international organization and I didn't want to disappoint her or embarrass myself.

"Every year the Foundation carries out its charitable and cultural works with a relatively low profile," Kathy continued. "But the announcement in January of King Faisal Foundation Prize winners creates interest around the world. The presentation of the awards each March puts the Foundation in the international spotlight."

Kathy gave me an autographed copy of her book, *Familiarity Breeds Content*, and asked if I'd consider writing a review for the *Saudi Gazette*. Of course, I agreed. Grateful for Kathy's willingness to help me feel more confident in this strange culture, I was more than willing to help her promote her book.

"By the way, I'm in a group of female writers living here in Riyadh, mostly Americans and Canadians. We take turns meeting in members' homes once a month for lunch and networking. You must join us next month."

Riding back to our compound, I wasn't nervous this time. Granted, I was placing my life in the hands of a strange man who was solely responsible for getting me back to our villa safely. I had no idea where I was, somewhere across the open desert on the periphery of Riyadh. Yet this time, my mind was preoccupied with positive thoughts about my afternoon with Kathy and meeting other Western female writers.

Less than a week later, the same Salah who asked me to be the English editor of *The Bulletin* left the office unexpectedly. Nobody seemed to know where he went or when he would return. Final approval and publication of *The Bulletin* would be delayed indefinitely because of his absence. Nobody, except for Mr. Al Senaidy, had the authority to make decisions and Mr. Al Senaidy was away indefinitely, too. I had no one to consult regarding *The Bulletin,* which I felt was my responsibility.

The freedom I felt earlier when Mr. Al Senaidy told me I could select articles to write and interviews to conduct was an illusion. If I couldn't be certain they would be approved and published, why bother?

To make matters worse, Ahmed, the young male Saudi on staff I considered a friend, put his by-line on an article I wrote. The article was about Al Taif, an ancient city in the Western region of Saudi Arabia, and it appeared in *The Bulletin* with Ahmed's name on it instead of mine. He was surprised when I told him what he did was plagiarism. He said in Saudi Arabia it was common practice.

I decided to take my complaints to Bill Towle, hospital administrator. Bill, an American, was sympathetic and regretted he could do nothing to help.

"Salah is related to head supervisor Dr. Al-Sharidah, so whatever he says goes," Bill said. "Here in Saudi Arabia, even among non-royals, who you know and who you're related to are far more important than what you know. As far as Ahmed putting his name on your article, forget it. That's not going to change."

Bill referred me to Munthir Kuzayli, deputy project director. Mr. Kuzayli, a Saudi, called me into his office.

"I understand you're frustrated, Mrs. Daugavietis," he said.

"Yes, I am," I answered. "I don't want to cause any problems but my job requires me to be in the hospital fifty hours a week. There's not enough work to do to keep me busy thirty hours a week."

What I wanted to tell him was it's impossible to publish a first-class monthly magazine for 3,000 employees on schedule and with content that informs, inspires and educates when there's no leadership. I also wanted to say as a woman, I have no authority to tell other people, including my superiors, what to do. I didn't say what was on my mind because I didn't know the boundaries for Western women expressing themselves.

"What would you like to do?" Mr. Kuzayli asked.

"I enjoy interviewing people and writing articles but I don't want to be in charge of *The Bulletin*. I want and need more time off so I can take better care of my husband."

A friend told me if I wanted time off from my job, I had to say because my husband needs more of my attention. Besides, Kathy Cuddihy might have some free-lance work for me. I didn't dare tell Mr. Kuzayli about Kathy, though.

"I see," he said.

"Also, because my husband is a physician and has a generous holiday and educational allowance for travel or medical conferences, I would like to go with him. I haven't been able to get my exit visa as easily as he does and that's a problem, too. What I would like is part-time status so I can be paid only for the hours I work."

Mr. Kuzayli kept looking at me, listening, hands clasped in front of him. I had his attention so I decided to continue.

"While I respect and am fond of my managers in Public Affairs, I want a connection with someone in Administration who has the authority to make decisions. I have no one in Public Affairs who can give me answers I need to do my job correctly and keep *The Bulletin* on schedule."

Mr. Kuzayli thanked me for my honesty and said I would hear from him after he had a chance to consider possible solutions to my problems.

Chapter 7

Cultural Differences

When Andy asked if I wanted to go to a beheading I said no.

"It's downtown, this Friday, at noon," he said. "If you change your mind, you'd better cover yourself, veil and all."

Covering my entire body in black—head, face, arms, legs, feet and hands—was bad enough; watching a person die in such a brutal way was repulsive. Then I remembered reading about a British journalist who disguised herself as a man, witnessed a beheading in Mecca and gained reputation as a fearless writer after describing the execution in her memoir. If she could do it, maybe I could, too, giving me credibility as a fearless writer myself. Andy, John and Bob would be proud of me—a possibility that pleased my ego.

First, I had to find the courage to go. When I mentioned my dilemma to Helen the next morning, she looked up from her desk with wide eyes.

"Can I go, too?" she said.

"You're not serious."

"Yes, I am. I've wanted to go for a long time but not as a single female. I've never been invited to go with a married couple. This is a rare opportunity I don't want to miss."

Helen was gutsier than I. She was Canadian and had been in the Kingdom for several years, whereas I was a relative newcomer. As head nurse in the V.I.P Ward, she knew how to handle Saudi males or anyone else who tried to usurp her authority. Having Helen along would give me courage.

"Helen and I are both going," I told Andy that evening.

"Good. We'll have to leave by ten-thirty," he said. "Two Pakistani drug dealers will be executed at noon in 'chop-chop square'."

Chop-chop square was a term expats used to describe the open space adjacent to the largest mosque in Riyadh where beheadings took place. An anesthesiologist Andy knew at the hospital, a Canadian, told him about the upcoming execution. This fellow was hired by authorities to sedate convicted criminals a day prior to beheading and drain enough blood to facilitate clean up. While many countries around the world impose the death penalty for convicted criminals, Saudi Arabia is one a few to hold public executions. In the Middle East, the death penalty is imposed for a variety of offenses including murder, rape, armed robbery, repeated drug use, adultery, witchcraft and others. In Saudi Arabia, public execution is beheading with a sword.

Helen stood by the curb in front of her apartment building when we pulled around the corner. Not wanting to attract attention, she wore her abaya but had her headscarf, veil and gloves rolled in a ball under her arm. As soon as we left the front gates of the compound, she and I covered our heads with scarves and adjusted our veils so we could see and breathe. We giggled nervously at each other, taking turns to check out our veiled images in the rearview mirror. As females, she and I were required to wear abayas outside of the compound but not scarves or veils, so this was a unique experience for us in more ways than one.

Vehicle traffic downtown was bumper-to-bumper with horns honking loudly. Males of all ages clogged the sidewalks and streets like a human tidal wave moving toward the mosque. Andy's colleague told him we could expect a big crowd—more than ten thousand perhaps. He wasn't exaggerating.

Andy parked the car while Helen and I stood on the sidewalk adjusting our sunglasses—not easy to do in 100-degree heat while wearing a black veil and gloves. We were the only females in sight, which made me feel uneasy. It was too late to turn back now. I didn't want to be a coward and back out even though I was beginning to feel like one.

Andy led the way as we merged into the crowd. Onlookers leaned out of second- and third-floor windows above the sidewalks, straining their necks for a better view, all while chanting Arabic phrases blaring from loud speakers on every corner. Up to this point, I knew nothing about beheadings. In my naivety, I had envisioned them taking place on a flag-draped dais, complete with podium and microphone so the master of ceremonies could explain to a subdued audience, perhaps seated in rows on folding chairs, who the criminals were and the crimes they had committed. For starters, this audience was anything but subdued, and from my vantage point, I saw no sign of a stage.

For Helen and me, covered completely in black, the heat was oppressive. The smell of sweaty bodies made me sick, especially after I realized I couldn't turn around. We were swept along, crammed together yet isolated from each other because of the deafening noise. I couldn't see because my sunglasses kept slipping and getting caught on my veil. Holding my veil tight against my face so I could look down without tripping, I had trouble breathing. As we moved toward an open area, I wanted to extricate myself from the pandemonium when the crowd began shouting, "Khalas. Khalas[16]."

Andy stopped in his tracks. I bumped against Andy and Helen bumped against me. I looked up to see a tall, black male wearing a white thobe, arms crossed, head wrapped in a turban, standing chest to chest in front of Andy and at least a foot taller.

"Get your women out of here," the man said, looking down at Andy with a stern demeanor. "It better for them."

"I'm leaving," I shouted to Andy.

---

[16] It's finished. It's finished.

I turned around and glanced down to see where I was stepping. Inches away, a pool of bright-red, shiny-wet blood caught my eye. A rumpled ghutra soaked with blood lay nearby. The guy in front of Andy was the executioner. I was standing near where two men had just died. I felt faint, but angry, too. Somehow, I rallied and grabbed Helen by the shoulders, turned her around and pushed her forward. She started hollering at someone close by.

"Get your cotton pickin' hands off me," she shouted.

I was horrified to see two Saudi males grinning stupidly at Helen's veiled form. I pushed her to the right and then forward with my hands on her back. I glanced behind me to make sure Andy was still there. If we had been separated, we never would have found each other. He came around in the lead and shouted to Helen and me to follow him back to the car.

"I was livid when that idiot grabbed my bum," fumed Helen. "These guys are out-of-their-minds crazy to touch a real woman. They sure picked the wrong one."

Thank goodness those guys who touched Helen weren't more aggressive because she would have fought back. A fistfight between Helen and two Saudi males would have landed us all in jail. To be honest, I was disgusted with myself for giving into my naïve curiosity about what it would be like to witness such a gruesome spectacle. I was disgusted with all the other spectators, as well, especially those who appeared to take pleasure observing the brutal, though hopefully painless, death of an allegedly "bad" person.

During the relatively brief time we lived in Saudi Arabia, I came to realize that Saudi culture was different, yet similar to our Western culture. We had practiced capital punishment in our country for years, although our methods for ending the life of a convicted criminal were not public as they were in Saudi Arabia. Granted, their justice system was swift, brutal and unforgiving with no chance for redemption. I wondered if innocent lives had been taken that day because of the Saudis' 'Old Testament' ways of punishment, "an eye-for-an-eye and a-tooth-for-a-tooth," based on Sharia or Islamic law. Before DNA testing became available, many convicted so-called criminals were executed in our country and later found innocent of their alleged crime.

Who's to say which culture is right and which is wrong? Either way, a life is taken to impose punishment. Expats criticized and poked fun at the Saudis. After all, I had done so, too. However, we had cultural ways in the U.S. that foreigners found distasteful and off-putting—for good reason.

Even though I didn't actually see a man die that day, I saw the immediate aftermath and couldn't get the sight of that bloodstained ghutra out of my mind. Lingering thoughts about the alleged criminals who died, their victims, the executioner who wielded the deadly sword—all of it disturbed me for weeks afterward.

~

Another less disturbing cultural practice I noticed after we came to Riyadh was the number of expats employing full-time housekeepers. Many families back home, including my own when I was a child, hired cleaning ladies, mostly African-American, one day a week to clean house and iron. Here, families employed live-in maids. Filipina maids mostly, but some were from the Sudan, Eritrea, Ethiopia and India. Most of these maids had passports; others did not. Most of the workers were treated with consideration but some were mistreated, depending on their employer. Some even died at the hands of their masters. An American friend, a female emergency room physician, told a heartbreaking story about a maid brought to the ER with life-threatening injuries, sustained through beatings by her master. Another maid attempted suicide by stabbing herself with scissors. Documented immigrants from other countries worked long hours for minimal pay. The lucky ones were able to return to their home countries once a year or every two years to visit their families.

Ahmed, my hairdresser at MC, charged 55SR ($15) for my monthly haircut that included a tip. He had a wife and two children back home in Sri Lanka where the family lived in a spacious and comfortable home. They employed a gardener, a cook and a housemaid. Ahmed proudly showed me photos of his family every time I came in for a haircut. I wondered how I would cope if I had to leave my family for a year at a time, sometimes two years, and then for only a two-week visit. For him, like many other workers in Saudi Arabia, it was a way of life.

One of the reasons our expat friends gave for having maids or servants made sense. Expat employers who earned generous salaries gave domestic workers a way to subsidize income from another job. Jobs in their naive countries were scarce and pay was less. Extra income earned here allowed immigrant workers to send money home to their families.

~

As we went about our weekly grocery shopping, Andy and I noticed other expats pushing grocery carts filled with large, clear plastic jerry cans, large containers of grape juice, empty beverage bottles, bags of sugar, yeast and plastic tubing.

"What *are* they doing with all that stuff?" I asked Andy.

"Making homemade wine."

"Isn't that illegal?"

"Yes, but most expats try it at least once. Some get good at it and make fairly decent wine."

Soon, Andy tried it, too, and we had a batch of red wine 'aging' in the crawl space under the stairs. When it was ready to drink two weeks later, I made labels by hand, naming the wine after our street: *La'Awzae* (pronounced 'lousy') ~ *1990, The Magic Kingdom of Saudi Arabia, 75% alcohol.* The stuff was so bad Andy lost interest after a while. I couldn't drink it because it gave me headaches. Whether or not the following story was true, we were told mutawa heard expats on compound were making wine. Word spread among expats that mutawa were coming to search all villas to arrest violators. Within hours, a significant number of expats had flushed the entire contents of their wine cellars down the toilets. The alcohol upset the bacterial flora in the compound's sewage treatment plant and blew the system, making it inoperable for a few days.

Some cultural differences were troubling to me: the beheading was one, and the number of workers from developing countries who lived on meager wages was another. The illegal brewing of beer and wine seemed humorous except when a worker from a developing country with no status was caught and punished by Sharia Law. Growing up, my dad told me not to go looking for trouble. My mother told me to keep my eyes and ears open and my mouth shut. I would be challenged to follow their advice as I began to question the validity of some of my long held beliefs about foreigners.

Chapter 8

Princesses' School

By late fall, our social life had improved. We knew more couples on and off the compound, and I enjoyed friendships with other expat employees at the hospital.

On one occasion, we were invited to a dinner party on compound hosted by one of Andy's Egyptian colleagues and his wife. Although it was a gathering for couples, the men were directed into one area of their spacious villa and the women into another. Each seating area had an elaborate buffet of Middle Eastern delicacies graced with enormous bouquets of fresh flowers. Among the offerings on the female side were large platters of lamb kebabs, rice, tabouli, grilled eggplant, stuffed grape leaves, hummus, dates, bread, fruit and sweets such as pistachio baklava, rice pudding and bananas wrapped in filo dough.

I sat next to Freda, whose husband Milt was a cardiologist. He was also Andy's boss as chairman of internal medicine. Natives of Greece, Freda and Milt had been at King Fahad since 1983.

Several weeks later, Freda and Milt invited us to their villa for a dinner party attended by couples from all over Riyadh. This time, the gathering seemed more Western. Andy and I ate with Elsie and Michael, a Lebanese couple who later became close friends. Michael entertained us with stories about challenges he experienced as an entrepreneur in Saudi Arabia. Founder and owner of an import business, he had to have a

Saudi partner or sponsor who automatically took 51 percent of the profits, even though Michael did most of the work.

Freda was an accomplished cook and hostess who prepared and served a sumptuous Greek dinner. A vivacious brunette, she was interesting to talk with and interested in what others had to say—a gracious and confident hostess. She didn't intend to intimidate me, but after she had told about her intact family background, I did feel awkward about Andy and me being middle-aged newlyweds. I also felt self-conscious about my lack of knowledge of the world at large. She seemed especially interested in what I did at the hospital and how I liked my work. I shared a few of my frustrations with her but tried to be circumspect. When Andy received a page to see a patient, I told Freda we had to leave.

"We had a wonderful evening," I said as she walked us to the door. "You have a beautiful home and lovely friends."

"I'm glad you could join us," she said, giving me a hug. "I must tell you, Pam—you need self-illumination. You have much to offer, but you seem so unsure of yourself."

While Freda's interest in me was flattering, her comment stung. At first, I couldn't imagine what she meant and then I felt embarrassed. I knew what she meant; she saw right through me. The façade of self-assurance I wore at these social gatherings was, in fact, transparent. All the other expats I had met were more educated, experienced and knowledgeable. Everyone besides me at Freda's party spoke two or three languages, including Andy who spoke Latvian. Still, I didn't want to admit my lack of confidence to Freda or allow my hurt and embarrassment to show. Instead, I hugged her back and smiled.

"Thank you, Freda, for a memorable evening."

~

Wednesday night before Thanksgiving, we were invited to Kathy and Sean's for dinner. Guests other than Andy and me were the general manager of the Marriott Hotel in Riyadh and his wife, John and Ellen; and Abdullah, a longtime and close Saudi friend of the Cuddihys. Andy and I mostly listened to the captivating conversation and stories these fascinating people were willing to share with us.

Abdullah, a well educated, well traveled, high-ranking government official, was married but did not bring his wife. Saudi custom restricts married couples from socializing in public with other married couples, whether Saudi nationals or expats. Abdullah was a gracious and elegant man and open about his views on at least some of his culture's customs. He even complained about his wife's "annoying veil." He had an impressive knowledge of fine wine, obviously garnered from direct experience, and he complained about mutawa "going crazy" downtown. When we asked about his falcons and horses, he told us he had 70 stable horses and 20 falcons. Someone asked what he had paid for the falcons, and he said between $500 and $250,000 each. He also told us that Prince Abdullah had more than 60 wives. Abdullah explained that multiple marriages were for political reasons to expand his family, since the Prince had no natural 'whole' brothers, meaning no brothers with the same mother and father.

John told us a story about a Swiss governmental delegation that stayed at the downtown Marriott Hotel. The manager in charge put up a Swiss flag in front of the hotel to welcome the visiting dignitaries. The Swiss flag has a white cross on it, which enraged the mutawa. They ripped down the flag, stormed the hotel, forced diners to leave the dining room and hassled female guests for being in mixed company without proper female Saudi attire.

John also told us the saga about an assistant manager in charge of the hotel while the regular manager was out of the country. The assistant manager ended up in jail for placing an advertisement in the local newspaper for "Saudi Champagne," a nonalcoholic beverage. John said when the regular manager learned what happened to his assistant, he disappeared and never returned to Saudi Arabia.

Hearing about Prince Abdullah's extravagances, the Swiss flag and the 'Saudi champagne' incidents gave us stories to share the next day. We attended a potluck Thanksgiving Dinner on the compound with three other American couples. The topic of conversation at expat gatherings, especially when all guests were American or Canadian, often focused on retelling 'Saudi stories' from either firsthand or secondhand experience. We loved entertaining each other with stories about the absurdities of Arabic culture.

"Nobody back home is much interested in what we've done and witnessed in Saudi Arabia," said Dick, our host. "Expats love to tell Saudi stories to each other for entertainment and education, especially for newcomers. Few back home will be interested unless they've had some connection to the Middle East. You may get their attention with a story or two, but that's it. You have to live and work here to appreciate the differences between our cultures and Saudi culture."

Thus, we sat down that late afternoon with new friends, who felt like old friends. We shared a feast of turkey, dressing, sweet potatoes, green beans, cranberry sauce, rolls, pumpkin and pecan pie. We talked about missing our families, yet how we felt fortunate to live in another culture. We were learning to get along with others whose beliefs and lifestyles were different, while better appreciating our own.

Later that evening, I told Andy that as different as I was from my Saudi colleagues and Muslim friends at the hospital in cultural ways, I was becoming increasingly aware we were the same in others.

"Even though Suhair is Muslim, and I'm Christian, she and I are alike in how we feel about our families, friends and life in general. We also talk about how we worship the same God even though our ways of worship are different."

"Maybe the people we've met at the hospital are more altruistic, or they wouldn't be working there," said Andy.

"You're probably right," I said. "Things may be different outside of our compound."

~

The following Wednesday, Freda called me at work.

"Pam, I'd like to meet with you tomorrow, here at our villa at 10:00 a.m. Are you available?"

"Yes, I can arrange it."

"Good. Very good. We must speak face-to-face, not over the phone. Bring a copy of your CV. My driver will pick you up at 9:50."

The next morning, Freda opened the front door with her usual verve, greeting me warmly with the customary two-cheek air-kiss and hug. She led me into her sunroom and motioned for me to sit in one of two chairs next to a round table covered with papers. Excusing herself, she returned moments later carrying a tray with two iced teas and a plate of biscuits and dates. She sat down in the chair next to mine and pulled herself up to the table.

"Everything we're about to discuss is strictly confidential," Freda said, pausing to look me in the eye. I nodded, but I was apprehensive about why we were meeting. I presumed it had to do with a writing assignment since she asked for my CV. She seemed serious. I preferred the more relaxed, whimsical Freda I had known socially the past month or so to this more business-like Freda.

"Two high-ranking Saudi princesses are opening a private, educational and cultural center for women and children in the Diplomatic Quarter," she said. "Our plan is to have sports activities and classes, as well as a cafeteria, boutique, and library. This initiative is the first of its kind ever attempted in the Kingdom. One princess is a daughter-in-law of King Fahad, and the other is a daughter of Prince Sultan, half-brother to King Fahad. Both are friends of mine who have hired me to be the project manager. I invited you here because I want you to be my assistant. Your official title is chairman of Public Affairs."

"Oh," I said, taken aback—stunned might be a better word.

I didn't know if I felt flattered or terrified. She handed me the organizational chart of the Al Manahil Center with my title circled in red. *Pamela Daugavietis, Chairman of Public Affairs,* appeared third from the top of the sheet, directly under Freda's as project manager. Freda was responsible only to the six-member board of directors, the two princesses and four other Saudi women, an American male legal advisor, and the male director of the Diplomatic Quarter.

"Of course, you'll quit your job at the hospital," she said, smiling. "No longer will you be working with Saudi males. Here, you'll be working with Saudi females. You'll report directly to me."

Freda was sounding as if I had already accepted the position. When I didn't respond, she gave me a bewildered look.

"Isn't that what you wanted?" she said. "You told me you wanted a job requiring your skills and talents without having to ask permission for every little decision you make."

She paused to look at me.

"Well, isn't it?"

"Yes, I guess so, but what about transportation?" I said. "I mean, I'd be off-compound, and I don't have a driver, and what about the legalities? The only reason for me to be in Saudi Arabia is because I'm married to Andy. I don't want to get him in trouble, or fired!"

I was stammering now and feeling panicky. Freda was growing impatient with my less than enthusiastic response.

"Pam, Pam, calm down," she said. "First of all, you'll ride with me every day. Secondly, you won't get in trouble. I wouldn't make you this offer unless I believed it was legal and that you could do the job."

I had so many questions I didn't know where to begin. I also was interested in Kathy Cuddihy's possible writing opportunities. Could I do both? Do I dare tell Freda about Kathy and what she and I discussed? If I took Freda up on her offer, I'd miss my first Riyadh writers group meeting. I wasn't even thinking of salary or compensation. I was more worried about spending five days a week away from the familiarity, safety and security of the hospital compound. I was also feeling anxious about all the secrecy and confidentiality surrounding this job.

I handed Freda my CV as she handed me a file filled with papers. Inside was an architectural drawing of all three floors of the school. She also included a copy of the administration flow chart, a list of classes and activities, my job description, and the school's mission and vision.

"Read all this over carefully and discuss what we talked about *only with Andy.* I can't emphasize enough how confidential this material is so *show it to no one*. In the meantime, I'll look over your CV. Can you meet again tomorrow morning at 8:30? My driver will pick you up at 8:15."

She glanced at her watch without waiting for me to answer.

"I have another appointment and you need to get to work. My driver will drop you off at the hospital."

That evening, I told Andy all about my meeting with Freda. I showed him the organizational papers and read my job description aloud.

"Write an announcement of the Center's opening. Write up general rules and regulations for the swimming pool and gymnasium. Create a membership application form. Write a letter of invitation to visit the center plus the invitation for the grand opening. Create an illustrated brochure describing the Center's facilities. Publish an artistically designed folder to contain all of the above. Prepare a detailed plan for the Opening Ceremony. Prepare a comprehensive plan of operation of your areas of responsibility, i.e., promotion and membership."

"Sounds exciting. You're going to take it, aren't you?"

"Exciting? It sounds overwhelming and impossible. They want it all completed by February—two months from now. It would be a huge undertaking with an experienced and cohesive team already in place, which the school doesn't have. I'm going to have to think this over carefully before I make a commitment."

"Why the hesitation? It sounds like a unique opportunity. I thought you'd be relieved to have an excuse to quit your job at the hospital."

I, too, was puzzled by my mixed feelings. True, my Saudi bosses had been challenging. True, I had complained about them, perhaps more than they deserved. When I read over my job description for the princesses' school, my irritations at work seemed inconsequential and petty, almost comical. Thinking of myself as chairman of Public Affairs for the Al Manahil

Center gave me pause. If I was over qualified and under appreciated at the hospital, I now felt over appreciated and under qualified to singlehandedly accomplish such a mandate. My background and lack of experience in the local culture didn't qualify me for such a responsibility. I still felt somewhat inept around Saudis and experienced expats. It made me nervous and mildly annoyed that Freda was talking as if I had already accepted her offer.

It was getting late. I decided to quit thinking about my job dilemma and read for a while before turning in. Next morning, I was pleasantly surprised to wake up feeling refreshed and more positive about Freda's offer. Andy told me whatever I decided was fine with him. He thought the offer sounded exciting, but it was up to me whether or not to accept. He reminded me that Freda asked me because she had confidence in me. Perhaps I needed to have more confidence in myself. Andy denied he was encouraging me to take the job because Freda's husband was his superior at the hospital. I believed him, but I did wonder if I would negatively affect Andy's career at the hospital by turning down the job.

Freda greeted me the next day with her usual verve and a big smile. She led me into their living room where the early morning sun gave everything in sight a golden, luminous glow.

"You sit closest to the window over there," she said, pointing to two overstuffed chairs overlooking the indoor-outdoor cactus garden. "I can't wait to hear what you've decided."

"No decision yet, Freda," I said.

Freda's smile faded.

"I'm still interested," I added quickly. "But there's a lot to consider, like what the job entails."

"Of course," she said, regaining her enthusiasm. "I'll take you to the school tomorrow. You must meet the other staff members. I also want you to meet one of the princesses."

One of the princesses? While thrilled and intrigued, I was also leery. I had never talked with a real princess before. What if she only spoke Arabic? The thought of meeting her pleased my ego but heightened my feelings of insecurity as a newcomer in the Kingdom. Unlike everyone, I was unfamiliar with commoners' rules of etiquette with royalty. Worse yet, if I turned Freda down, would her husband take it out on Andy since Milt was Andy's boss?

Back at my office, I waited until Suhair and Hala left the office for their mid-morning break. I dialed Munthir Kuzayli's extension and spoke with his secretary. She arranged for me to meet with him briefly at 11:00. When I entered his office, he stood and greeted me with a welcoming smile. Mr. Kuzayli was Saudi, but he always wore a Western business suit and never the traditional Saudi male thobe and ghutra.

"My situation in Public Affairs hasn't improved since I spoke with you a while ago," I said. "I'm considering another job offer, outside the compound."

"What kind of a job offer?" he asked.

A look of displeasure replaced his welcoming smile.

"I'm not at liberty to say."

Straightening his posture, he sat down and pulled himself up to his desk. He clasped his hands together, paused, and cleared his throat before speaking.

"It's illegal for you to work without an igama," he said, thumping his hands on the desk when he said 'illegal'. "My advice is to stay at the hospital. If you decide to accept the other job, I warn you—*proceed with caution.*"

Breathless after hurrying back to my office, my hands shook as I dialed Freda's number.

"Munthir Kuzayli says I can't work outside the hospital compound. He said I don't have an igama, and besides, I . . ."

"Pam, Pam, slow down," Freda said. "Take a breath. You worry too much. I assure you, you have the princesses' protection. My driver will pick you up at 8:30 tomorrow morning."

The princesses' protection? Is that like having a fairy godmother? I believe in angels and spooks but princesses with magic powers? Later on that evening, when I told Andy about my meeting with Mr. Kuzayli and what Freda said, he shrugged.

"What about the stories we've heard?" I wailed. "I'm in a car crash, and they take my driver to the ER, but I'm left to die because Saudi males aren't allowed to touch females. What if they don't believe me when I tell them I have the princesses' protection? If I'm unconscious, what proof do I have? A tattoo on my forehead?"

"We don't know if that story is true," he said.

Fear of the unknown caused me to project my anxiety on Andy. I would be leaving the security of the compound every day without him to protect me. Another concern was my limited ability to speak Arabic and my lack of experience navigating the culture as a Western female. While I hadn't been asked to sign a contract yet, I knew I would soon be forced to choose between my job at the hospital job and a job with the princesses. Working for Saudi princesses breaking away from tradition to open a co-ed school sounded exciting yet scary. I tried to stop obsessing about it until my visit to the school the next day when I would meet the princess herself.

With Freda's credentials, we had no trouble getting through the heavily guarded front gate of the Diplomatic Quarter. Freda's driver dropped us off at the school—a modern structure surrounded by neatly manicured landscaping. Our appointment was at 10:00. The austere and deserted building with few windows felt more like an oversized mausoleum than a school as we made our way down the long marble corridor.

"Freda, I'm nervous."

"Don't be silly."

The sharp staccato sound of her high heels hitting the marble floors echoed through the empty hallway.

"But I'm not sure . . ."

"You're fine. Just be yourself."

Be myself? I wasn't sure which part of me had agreed to be there that day. Was it the part of me that became furious when Ahmed put his name on an article I wrote for *The Bulletin*, and when Salah told me I was wrong about an error he had made? I had complained to Freda about the downside of working with Saudi men with little or no experience publishing the hospital's monthly newsletter. What's more, they wouldn't take my suggestions for making it better. After all, I'm just a female. Perhaps Freda was simply trying to help me find a job where I could use my skills without having to cope with male bosses.

The other me was still a naive newcomer to Riyadh. I wasn't a prominent member of the international social scene as Freda had been the past seven years. Freda's vitality and good looks dazzled me when I met her a few weeks earlier. I was impressed by her connections and reputation among the expat community. My ego loved the positive comments she made about the articles I was writing for the hospital. Perhaps I had complained too much about Mr. Al Senaidy's management style and my frustrations with my other male colleagues. I never dreamed she would offer me a job at a school founded by Saudi princesses. Flattered at first, I was now sinking into fear and feelings of inadequacy.

Like an obedient subordinate, I followed Freda into the conference room. I wanted desperately to make a good impression so the princess would approve of me being Freda's assistant. I was startled when I caught sight of her, just four feet away, seated in the middle of the far side of a large, long wooden table. She looked nothing like the caricature I had imagined—a pampered and heavily made-up princess dripping with jewels, ordering servants around, eating dates out of a solid-gold dish. Instead, she was a beautiful, fresh-faced young woman who seemed relaxed, almost ordinary in appearance and sincerely pleased to see us.

"Hello, Pam. Thank you for agreeing to meet with us today," the princess said.

Surprised by her warmth and sincerity, I simply responded, "You're welcome."

She wore no hijab; a paisley-patterned shawl covered her shoulders. Her long black hair was pulled back from her face, and her dark eyes were kind and expressive. Her skin was flawless. She had fine features, a gracious smile, and a soft, melodic voice.

"We hope you will consider joining us here at the school. We would be pleased to have someone with your background and credentials involved with us in this important undertaking."

I was tempted to look over my shoulder to see who she was talking to, thinking it couldn't possibly be me.

"I have confidence in Freda, and she certainly has confidence in you," the princess continued. "As you know, education for both girls and boys is extremely important. We want to make sure the next generation of young people in our country is ready for the many changes taking place here in the Middle East, as well as around the world."

The princess paused and then asked if I had any questions. Either out of shock, shyness or a lack of self-confidence, I simply said no. Freda thanked the princess, and we excused ourselves and left the room. Our scripted meeting with the princess lasted only a few moments, but her modesty and sincerity impressed me. I also liked her determination to be a trailblazer in a culture that suppressed women. In my mind, I continued to obsess about what to tell Freda. If I say yes, my boys will be impressed that I'm working at a premier, co-ed school in Riyadh, run by Saudi princesses—an historic first. Perhaps the folks back home who thought I was crazy to follow Andy to the desert would be jealous once they found out about my exciting new career.

"What do you think?" Freda asked once we were down the hallway.

"I liked the princess's sincerity."

"So you'll accept the job?"

"I don't know, Freda. What if I can't meet your expectations of me?"

I realized Freda herself was a force to be reckoned with—not exactly like Mr. Al Senaidy, but an intimidating force nonetheless.

"The only one who doubts that you can is you," she said.

~

The next morning, I called Freda to tell her I'd accept the job. First, I had to write my resignation letter to Mr. Al Senaidy and lie about why I was leaving. If the mutawa found out about the school, they'd shut it down before it opened. I dreaded telling him because I was beginning to like the man, even though he frustrated me at times. If I take the job at the school, he'll be angry with me and Andy's reputation at the hospital could be affected. If I don't take the job, Freda will be angry with me and her husband will be angry with Andy. When I walked into Mr. Al Senaidy's office the next morning, I was surprised when he greeted me warmly. Perhaps he wasn't upset after all. The moment I sat down, he reached for a sheet of paper on his desk and began waving it in the air.

"What's this, Pam?" he said, frowning at me and shouting. "I don't believe you want to leave us. Tell me you've changed your mind."

"It hasn't been an easy decision, Mr. Al Senaidy. My third-month anniversary is coming up the 26th of this month. I read in my contract that I can resign, or you can let me go without any explanation up to the 26th."

"Well, then," he said, "I refuse to accept your resignation. I told Nabiha to return it to Munthir Kuzayli indicating that your resignation has no validity. We need you here."

With that, he left his office, put my resignation letter on Nabiha's desk and walked out of the Public Affairs Department.

Mr. Al Senaidy's response to my letter of resignation was startling. I couldn't believe he wouldn't accept it. Would he have understood my decision if he had known I'd be working with a real princess? Six months ago, I worried about not having a suitable job in Saudi Arabia. Now it seemed, I had two.

Freda and her driver picked me up at 8:30 Monday morning for my first day at the Al Manahil Center. The day began with a meeting of the board of directors to go over my job description and determine priorities. I recognized the board members as the same women I met earlier when I met the princess, although the princess wasn't there. One by one, the women said everything on the list they gave me was a priority. They said I should jump in and do whatever needed to be done.

Next, I met with Mr. Samy, the accountant, to discuss pay and hours. I was surprised to learn my pay at the school was less than at the hospital. Mr. Samy said my pay would increase as my value to the school increased. In other words, I had to prove myself beyond the credibility of my résumé and Freda's endorsement. As soon as my meeting with Mr. Samy ended, I returned to my office and organized my desk.

The scene before me was oddly reminiscent of my first day as sole proprietor of Professional Business Services in Petoskey. There, I had a one-woman operation that operated on a shoestring. Here in Riyadh, nine years later, I had the same basic equipment and similar challenges. I had a phone, a typewriter, a file cabinet with no files in it, no supplies, no contacts to call. In Petoskey, the challenge was staying afloat financially. Here, it was meeting the unreasonable expectations of others.

By the end of that first day, I had set up a filing system and created a calendar so I could keep a log of my hours and activities. On Tuesday, I re-organized my desk, typed up the rules and regulations, and proctored a typing test for several secretarial job applicants. On Wednesday, I re-organized the hanging file system and typed up the dress code and index cards of department heads with phone numbers. At the end of the day, I had also typed up a description of classes for boys and girls. Exhausted from doing busywork, I was more than ready for the weekend. I went home that night feeling useless and discouraged. Moments after I walked in the door, the phone rang.

"Pam, we all want you to come back," said Mr. Al Senaidy, sounding both cordial and contrite. "We need you in Public Affairs. Can you be in my office on Saturday morning at 9:00 a.m.?"

"Yes, yes, I can," I heard myself say.

Freda called mid-morning the next day.

"Freda, I am so sorry to tell you, but I can't continue at the school."

"Pam, why? What happened?"

"Nothing you or anyone at the school did," I assured her. "Mostly, I don't feel comfortable being away from the hospital compound all day. Besides, the job exceeds my abilities to execute it as well as it deserves to be executed, especially with such a tight deadline."

Freda told me she was disappointed, but she understood. She said she was sorry and wished me well. Of course, I told her the same and thanked her for her confidence in me. I apologized for backing out but told her the school would be better served by having someone more socially connected in the expat and Saudi communities and knowledgeable about the Saudi culture.

After we hung up, I thought about what Freda told me after our first meeting. She said I needed self-illumination. She was right. For all the anxiety and frustration this experience caused me, I was beginning to see my quandary as a gift in disguise. Ambivalent at first, in the end I listened to that 'still, small voice' within and told the truth. I did what I felt was best for me, not to please Freda, nor the princess, nor Mr. Al Senaidy, nor Andy. I didn't want to be chairman of Public Affairs at the Al Manahil Center, as impressed as I was with the princess and her passion for educating Saudi children. I wanted to be Andy's wife and a writer for King Fahad National Guard Hospital's Public Affairs. At this time in my life, that was more than enough. I had been gone from the office only seven days, yet my colleagues in Public Relations welcomed me back as if I had been away for months. Suhair, Nabiha and Hala told me they missed me and gave me hugs. Even the men, Mr. Al Senaidy, Ahmed, Abdullah, and Falah, greeted me with smiles and told me how relieved they were to have me back.

My colleagues in Public Affairs were the only ones at the hospital who knew I had quit, although none of them knew the real reason. If anyone asked what caused me to change my mind, I said Mr. Al Senaidy allowed me to have flexible hours so I could work in Public Affairs and take better care of my husband. Everyone else most likely never knew I was gone.

As I went about my usual routine at the hospital, I saw the hospital—and its staff— through new eyes. I felt more 'at home' than before. The hospital was where I belonged, and not at the princesses' school, even though I admired their mission. Here at King Fahad National Guard Hospital, I had interviewed many of the people who were now waving and smiling at me as I passed them in the hallway. I had listened to nurses, doctors, technicians, housekeepers, food service workers, and maintenance staff tell why they came to Saudi Arabia to work. They had shared their stories with me about how they missed their families back home and their frustrations at work, yet they loved their jobs. I could relate to all their stories. I valued the cultural, ethnic and religious diversity and the congeniality of the people who made this hospital what it was—a place of compassion, healing and hope. I realized that by being here with Andy, half a world away from our families and home——I was feeling more 'at home' within myself.

Chapter 9

Christmas in Riyadh

When Mr. Al Senaidy met with me to go over my new working arrangements, he said he would pay me for the seven days of work I'd missed. I was astonished. When I told him Andy and I were planning a five-day trip to Bahrain between Christmas and New Year's, and a three-week trip home to the U.S. in January, I expected at least some pushback. Instead, he said, "No problem." We negotiated a new contract giving me days off when I wanted and the freedom to work from home. I would receive pay only for the time I worked, which is what I preferred. I wanted to hug him, but, of course, I didn't. Instead, I shook his hand with both of my hands, bowed my head in a gesture of respect, and told him how grateful I was for his understanding and generosity. He seemed embarrassed but pleased.

With less than a month to schedule interviews and write articles for the January issue of *The Bulletin* before we left, I would have plenty to keep me busy at work. It was time to write our Christmas letter to everyone back home. Mail service to the U.S. was unpredictable, so I wanted our families and friends to hear from us in time for them to write back. This year, more than ever before, I *needed* to receive Christmas cards. Just thinking about Christmas, now only three weeks away, brought conflicting emotions—gnawing homesickness, yet joyful expectation.

I was missing John and Bob terribly, as well as other family members, but I was also missing the visible signs of Christmas. We had no twinkling lights, no nativity scenes, no images of angels, Santa Claus, elves or Rudolph. Christmas in Saudi Arabia was illegal. Our Christian friends on compound warned us to be discreet with decorations. Andy and I didn't have decorations to put up, other than a few ornaments we bought in Turkey. We had no Christmas lights, no Christmas tree, no Christmas songs on tape to play at home or in the car.

Several days after I returned to the hospital, I bumped into Janet, my good friend and neighbor who worked as a secretary for a trauma surgeon.

"What are you and Andy doing for Christmas?" she asked.

"Bahrain between Christmas and New Year's but no special plans for Christmas Day. It's on a Monday this year so we'll both be working.

"Dick and I will be in Wisconsin for a month to visit our kids and grandkids. We won't be using our artificial tree this year. It's small but has lights and ornaments. You're welcome to use it."

Dick and Janet lived in the next block on Al Awzae Street, so Dick dropped off the little tree later that evening. It reminded me of Charlie Brown's Christmas tree, humble yet cheerful and heartwarming. I always looked forward to watching *A Charlie Brown Christmas* on TV every year with John and Bobby when they were little. The story line, as I remembered, was Charlie's concern that Christmas was becoming too commercialized. He told Linus he was getting depressed because consumerism and frantic activity had overshadowed the true meaning of Christmas. Perhaps our little tree would help remind me of what Charlie Brown was trying to say to Linus without sounding too religious. Christmas is a time to reflect on God's love for humanity through Jesus' birth. I realized that Andy and I were now living not far from Bethlehem—only 800 miles by car and two hours by plane. The thought of it gave me comfort. Other than where we were in Turkey, we were closer to where Jesus was born than at any other time in our lives. I tried to think about that rather than how far away we were from our loved ones.

We set up our tree on an end table in our second-floor family room. Every night after work, I would run upstairs and turn on the lights to see the cheerful glow they cast throughout the darkened room. Just like back home, daylight hours in the desert diminished as winter approached. Outside temperatures had dropped into the 50s and 60s Fahrenheit, but we had no snow—only sand, lots and lots of sand.

We bought several "winter" tapes by Boney M in the hospital gift shop, hoping for some familiar seasonal music. I was thrilled when we listened to the tapes. They contained many of our favorite Christmas songs, both secular and religious. We realized the cassette's secular label that read "winter tape" was to conceal religious music that would be illegal.

My mood gradually improved as each day brought new surprises. Kathy called to tell me the *Saudi Gazette* had published my book review. I finally had a by-line in a local newspaper although I never received a check for writing it. Christmas cards were starting to come from home. We also received a few invitations to holiday parties off and on the compound. Freda's females-only Christmas party at her villa was one of them. She had invited 50 women living in Riyadh who represented a dozen countries around the world. We danced and sang to Christmas songs while enjoying Freda's sumptuous spread of Greek hors d'oeuvres and sweets.

On Christmas Eve, we attended a festive progressive dinner hosted by three couples, all staff physicians and their wives, all Canadians. As soon as we came home that night, we turned on our Charlie Brown Christmas tree and took turns reading the Christmas story aloud from the Bible my Grandmother Harman gave me. I could feel the Christmas spirit more than ever that night, remembering the joys of Christmases past.

Growing up in Worthington in the '40s and '50s, Christmas was more about celebrating the birth of Jesus and spending time with family and friends. We gave each other simple, handmade gifts rather than store-bought gifts. In spite of all the changes that had taken place in my life the past ten years, the adjustments, the fears and anxieties, the death of my father two years earlier, my homesickness for my boys and family, I also felt deep gratitude and peace. Andy was here with me, and we were happy together.

Christmas morning was a business-as-usual day, except it felt special, magical even, as Christmas always does to me. Every morning at the breakfast table, Andy and I took turns reading from *Daily Word*, an inspirational magazine I had subscribed to for years. On this December 25th, I thought about our families gathered around their Christmas trees back home as I read, *"I am grateful for all the love I have experienced and all I have to share. I remember those who have taught me, guided me, and loved me."*

My consolation was the anticipation of going home in January to see everyone face to face, to give them hugs and hear all about what they had been doing in our absence. Andy and I drove down to the hospital with our windows rolled up as our Boney M tape played loudly. We entered the hospital through the side door and made our way through the front lobby, devoid of any signs of Christmas or holiday celebration and deserted except for one maintenance worker sweeping the floor.

"The Saudis must know this is a holy day for us," I said. "The place is empty."

Just then, several Filipino maintenance workers walked past us.

"Merry Christmas," they whispered, smiling broadly. We returned their greetings as well as their smiles.

Andy and I waved as we parted ways. His office was down another hallway, on the other side of the hospital. I saw Walter, a Filipino maintenance man, emptying wastebaskets in Ward 15.

"Christmas is Christ," he called out softly.

"He's always here, in our hearts," I said, forgetting for a moment that at King Fahad, Christmas was illegal.

Walter's simple greeting stayed with me all day. Christmas may be illegal here, but the Christ Spirit is everywhere, at all times, and within everyone, whether they are aware of it or not.

One inside Ward 16, I walked down the hall from my office to make a cup of coffee. Miss Lily, a Filipina housekeeper, slipped quietly into the kitchenette and closed the door. She stepped next to me without saying a word. Older than I by a few years, and a foot shorter, Miss Lily had worked at King Fahad Hospital for nine months.

"Merry Christmas, Miss Lily," I said. "How are you doing?"

"I miss my children," she said, looking up at me with tears in her eyes. "They all back home in the Philippines. They so far away."

"Oh, I know what you mean," I said, wrapping my arms around her. "Let's pray for them and each other as we focus today on the true meaning of Christmas. I just saw Walter down the hall and he greeted me with, 'Christmas is Christ.' He reminded me that the true meaning of Christmas is love. You send loving thoughts to your family in the Philippines, and I'll send loving thoughts to our families in the U.S."

We hugged once again before Miss Lily left the kitchenette without making a sound, just as she came.

At lunch, I heard a Canadian secretary say the hospital needed blood donations. I stopped by the lab on my way back to my office to see if I qualified. I had tried to donate in the past, but my blood pressure was too low.

This time, my blood pressure was 100 over 60. They accepted me as a donor, and I gave a pint of blood for the first time in my life—my Christmas present to an unknown recipient.

On my way back to my office, I passed through the Family Medicine Clinic. An Egyptian nurse, wearing a hijab, handed me a wrapped plate of Christmas cookies tied with a bow. "Merry Christmas," she said, even though she was Muslim.

"Thank you so much. Merry Christmas to you."

I accepted the cookies gratefully, even though we had more than enough holiday sweets at home. Further down the hall, I caught sight of the shy, slightly built, toothless Bangladeshi flower vendor wearing a white cloth wrapped around his head and a long yellow cloth around his neck. Every day he sat in the same place, near the entrance to the Emergency Department, selling fresh flowers. He didn't speak English, and I never bought anything from him, but he was always friendly to me. As I passed his stand, he smiled broadly—his white teeth in stark contrast to the dark color of his skin. With one hand he offered me a long-stemmed red rose, with the other he handed me a Christmas tree ornament—a small, red bird sitting in a golden cage. Surprised by these unexpected gifts, I thanked him in English and offered him the plate of Christmas cookies from the Egyptian nurse. He took the cookies, smiled, bowed and waved to me as I continued down the hall.

That evening, we went to Carol and Martin's for Christmas dinner. It was Carol's birthday, so we had birthday cake after a delicious meal of standing rib roast, baked potatoes, cranberry sauce, broccoli and glazed carrots. Carol and Martin's son Chris was there from Canada along with friends of theirs, another Canadian physician and his wife. Even though we had known Carol and Martin for only five months, they had become good friends. Our dinner together was the perfect ending to what turned out to be a perfect Christmas, in spite of my reservations three weeks earlier.

Later that evening, Andy and I opened our Christmas cards to each other as we listened to our Boney M tape. We lit our candle from Mary's House long enough to say prayers for our family because we wanted to save it for Christmases to come. Instead of giving each other a gift this year, we agreed to spend our money on our trip to Bahrain between Christmas and New Year's, and our trip to the U.S. in January. In spite of being far away from home, our first Christmas in Saudi Arabia and our first as husband and wife was definitely a Charlie Brown Christmas. We had few decorations, a simple tree, and no presents. Still, I was filled with the same Christmas Spirit I remembered from my childhood—feelings of mystery and wonder, peace and joy, and most of all, gratitude and love.

~

The day after Christmas, we flew from Riyadh to Manama, the capital of Bahrain, where the weather was idyllic every day—perfect for walking and window-shopping. I loved not having to wear an abaya, and being able to walk the streets holding hands with my husband. The Kingdom of Bahrain is an island in the Persian Gulf, connected to Saudi Arabia by the King Fahad Causeway. Although an Arab nation, social and religious dictates are less stringent than in Saudi Arabia, perhaps because Bahrain was becoming a global financial center and tourist destination.

Downtown Manama was a modern city of high-rise buildings surrounded on three sides by sandy beaches, public parks, and walkways. Swaying palm trees lined the boulevard along the shore of the Persian Gulf. Although many enticing shops sold upscale clothing, jewelry, rugs and sweets, our only purchases were several baskets woven by local artisans.

Besides not having to wear an abaya and holding hands in public, highlights of our five-day stay in Manama included eating bacon for breakfast, drinking wine with dinner and sipping real champagne at midnight on New Year's Eve. I've never been a huge fan of bacon but knowing pork was illegal in Saudi Arabia whetted my appetite for it. Andy and I had bacon and eggs every morning.

After a relaxing time away in a less culturally strict Arab country, I was surprised to be searched by airport security in Bahrain when Andy and I flew back to Riyadh. Male guards took my purse and sent me into a small area completely enclosed with heavy drapery while a female guard frisked me from top to bottom. I wasn't asked to take off any clothing, but she felt every inch of my body through the clothes I was wearing. Mildly annoyed by the unexpected pat down, I became even more annoyed when I stepped out of the enclosed area to see the security guard rifling through my purse. He took out my small change purse where I carried a small cross I received years ago at the Presbyterian Church in Petoskey. The guard took the cross out of my purse, held it up like a trophy and showed it around in a mocking way to the other security guards. All of them chuckled and snickered.

"Give me that," I said as I snatched the cross out of his hand. "You had no right to take that out of my purse. I wasn't displaying my cross openly. I respect your traditions as Muslims and I expect you to respect mine as a Christian. Thank you."

My boldness surprised the guards who stood there staring at me. My boldness surprised even me. After I gathered up my purse and my carry-on, I looked at the guard who had searched my purse.

"Is that all?" I said.

He nodded and waved me through security.

After we returned from Bahrain and before we left for the U.S., Kathy called me at work to wish me a Happy New Year.

"Pam, I'm up to my eyeballs with all the planning for the Faisal Foundation Prizes this year. Are you still willing to help me?"

"Absolutely. When do I start?"

"Not until the end of February."

"We get back from the U.S. on February 12th. Allowing for a few days to recover, I should be ready to work on the 17th. I'll call you as soon as we get back."

~

Our first trip home to the U.S. in January and February exceeded our expectations. We covered four states and seven cities or towns—Tallahassee, Florida; Grand Haven, Ann Arbor, Hillsdale, and Petoskey, Michigan; Worthington, Ohio; and Winnetka, Illinois. We spent quality, although brief, one-on-one time with our parents, our children, and my two sisters. We met our future daughter-in-law, Amy Schaefer, for the first time. Andy and I liked her immediately. John said they were just friends, but I had a feeling she was 'the one.' When we drove to Petoskey, Bob and several of his friends surprised us by decorating our motel room with crepe paper streamers and a huge welcome-home sign. Thanks be to God everyone was healthy and doing well in our absence.

We were away for three weeks, but the days flew by quickly. It was tough coming back to Riyadh because I knew it would be months before we'd see everyone again. I also had serious jet lag. Having the Faisal Foundation Prize writing assignments to look forward to eased my re-entry. Had I known about the special visitor to our VIP Ward on my first day back, I might have been more excited than I was when our alarm went off at 6:00 Saturday morning.

Chapter 10

Prince Abdullah's Visit

Ward 16 was bustling with activity when I walked through the doors at 7:00 a.m. Housekeeping staff scurried here and there with brooms, mops, and dust rags. In the nursing station, security guards with flashlights peeked behind doors, in drawers and under desks and chairs.

"What's going on here?" I asked Tav, the Filipino server carrying a breakfast tray to a patient down the hall.

"Prince Abdullah is coming today," he said with a big smile. "Everyone is excited."

Prince Abdullah, head of the Saudi Arabian National Guard (SANG), and younger half-brother of King Fahad, would be visiting his nephew, a patient in Suite 4, just steps away from my office.

Mid-morning, two Saudi Arabian National Guard security officers came to our door and spoke in Arabic to Suhair. They told her that she, Hala and I had to stand by our office door while they searched under our desks. They looked in all the drawers with metal detectors and flashlights but found nothing suspicious. First, they told Suhair we had to stay in our office. We weren't allowed to leave the ward until after the prince left. Then, they told us we had to keep our door closed. Later, they gave us permission to stand in the doorway when the prince came. Hala, who was pregnant, left the department. She wasn't keen to put up with all the rules about staying in our room, access to the cafeteria and bathroom privileges. All entrances to Ward 16 were locked; armed guards stood at all exits and doors. Suhair and I settled in for the duration with eager anticipation, patiently waiting for the show to begin.

Sometime later, one of the guards told Suhair that Prince Abdullah wouldn't come until after the noon prayer. The morning had flown by without accomplishing much work. We were hungry and tired of waiting. At this point, with a lockdown in place, we had no choice but to stay. The head of security hurried down the hall making sure all closet and utility room doors were locked. The hospital's medical director appeared around the corner, and then disappeared into the royal nephew's suite, presumably to offer his assistance. Mr. Al Senaidy came rushing down the hall waving an incense burner up and down, wafting fragrant fumes in the air. Helen came hurrying down the hall from the other direction with a scowl on her face.

"Mohammed, get rid of that incense burner right now," she hollered. "You'll set off the fire alarm, and that's all I need."

Mr. Al Senaidy gave her a sheepish grin and left the ward with his incense burner, chastened. Like a mother hen protective of her brood, Helen kept a tight rein on activities in Ward 16. She didn't want its soothing environment compromised by Prince Abdullah's visit.

At 12:35 p.m., the first of five Filipinos entered through the main doorway one after the other, each pushing his own large, double-decker cart. One by one, armed SANG guards wearing white gloves and full-dress uniforms searched every cart. The first three carts contained numerous stainless-steel domes covering dishes emitting aromas suggesting hot foods. Next came two more carts with giant baskets of fruit: grapes, pears, apples, peaches, plums, bananas, and dates. Soon, a florist and his two assistants appeared with three carts. The first two carts carried huge bouquets of flowers. We counted a dozen birds of paradise in one bouquet. The last cart carried a gargantuan arrangement of red roses—the largest floral display I had ever seen. Guards searched all carts and floral displays from top to bottom.

At 1:00 p.m., an announcement over the loudspeaker ordered drivers of vehicles in the V.I.P. parking lot to move their cars. Miss Lily wiped baseboards at the end of the hallway with one hand while keeping a steady eye on the unfolding drama. Like the rest of us, she didn't want to miss anything. She wanted to appear busy rather than stand, stare and wait. After she worked her way down the hall, she approached our door, stepped close to Suhair and me and spoke in a whisper.

"I will always remember this day because I'm going to see Prince Abdullah. I am fortunate. I'm from the Philippines, and I'm going to see the Crown Prince of Saudi Arabia."

Suhair rolled her eyes and shrugged.

"It's exciting to see all these important people, including the prince," I said to Suhair. "It isn't every day that His Royal Highness Prince Abdullah comes to visit."

"In God's eyes, he's no better than anyone else," she said in a somber tone of voice. "We are all equal before God."

Mr. Kuzayli and Dr. Al-Sharidah, supervisor general, entered the hallway through the doors leading from the main hallway. They chatted a few minutes with security guards before entering Suite 4. Mr. Kuzayli smiled at me as they passed by our office. I assumed he was pleased to see I was back at work. At 1:30 p.m., another SANG soldier appeared to tell us the prince would arrive in 30 minutes.

"Talateen dagiga[17]," he repeated as he walked briskly down the hall.

Half kidding, I told Suhair it would be exciting if the prince would

---

[17] Thirty minutes.

see us standing here and walk over to say hello. Suhair, who never veiled but always covered her hair at work, laughed out loud.

"We should all be wearing veils," she said with sarcasm. "Besides, he doesn't shake hands with females. Ridiculous."

Suhair scoffed at Saudi culture forbidding males from touching non-related females, forcing females to veil and other excessive restrictions, a view I came to realize was shared by other Middle Eastern expats. It seemed Suhair wasn't impressed as Miss Lily and I were by Prince Abdullah's visit.

The hospital administrator and the nursing supervisor, both Americans, entered Suite 4. By now, it was nearly 2:00 p.m. All I could think about was getting something to eat and finding a bathroom; still, I didn't want to miss the grand finale. Seconds later, Prince Abdullah entered the ward wearing a red-and-white-checked ghutra and a full-length white cape trimmed with gold braid over his thobe. A head taller than any of the entourage of SANG officers surrounding him, he led the group in tight formation, all staring straight ahead, all wearing flowing tan capes trimmed in gold. His mustache and goatee were so black and well defined they didn't look real. A Saudi male stood outside the door to Suite 4 awaiting the prince. They greeted each other with the typical male handshake, kissing once on the right cheek, twice on the left, followed by more handshaking and more kissing. After preliminary greetings, both men turned and entered the suite, the prince leading the way. Two armed guards snapped to attention as the door closed. No more than five minutes later, Prince Abdullah emerged from Suite 4, surrounded by the same SANG officers, all striding in formation toward the back entrance to Ward 16.

By the time we arrived at work the next day, the nephew had checked out. Suhair and I surmised he went home to get some rest. All the hoopla of his uncle's five-minute visit no doubt exhausted him as it had us.

The following Wednesday, I hosted our group of Western female writers for a morning get-together at our villa. With my new working arrangement at the hospital, I had no problem asking for a few hours off that morning although I didn't give a specific reason. Kathy Cuddihy, the group's founder, had already told me she couldn't attend. We had no dues, no by-laws, no officers or organization of any kind. Several days before the get-together, I typed up a list of all 16 members with names, locations and phone numbers. I wanted to make sure I had everyone accounted for before I started calling to confirm if they were coming. I did this as a convenience for all our members to keep track of one another. What I didn't know was that organized groups for females were illegal in Saudi Arabia.

The closest publication we had to a telephone book was a small pamphlet distributed by the hospital with compound phone numbers only. Expats and locals living on other compounds networked at social events and exchanged business cards or scribbled addresses and telephone numbers on scraps of paper. I figured I would be doing a favor by sending everyone a copy of the typed list of names with contact information. The first few women I called on the phone objected so strongly I ripped up the printed lists I had ready to mail. Members feared reprisals from the 'authorities' for breaking the law. If the list got out somehow and fell into the wrong hands, we could all be in trouble.

Still, I had to make a list of names for security so everyone could get into the compound. I telephoned the day before to notify security staff of my 'ladies tea'. I told them my husband would drop off the list at the front gate on his way to work the next morning. As it turned out, only eight women showed up. Those who couldn't make it missed a lively discussion. We mostly compared Saudi stories, aired frustrations, offered each other support and validation, and shared laughter and heartwarming camaraderie. All our members were living in Saudi Arabia because of their husbands' careers and not their own, although most of them were professional writers. Their drivers dropped them off and waited at the curb until the meeting was over.

That weekend, our Canadian friends Don and Millie-Lynn invited us to go on a desert picnic. Millie-Lynn brought marinated lamb kebabs and baklava, everyone's favorite Middle Eastern sweet made with nuts, filo dough and honey. Andy and I brought an assortment of Middle Eastern side dishes we picked up at a local deli, including hummus, baba ghanouge (eggplant), and tabouli (bulgur wheat with parsley, mint, onion, garlic and tomato).

We made our way into the desert lowlands in Don's four-wheel-drive Subaru. We set up camp, put out folding chairs and a cooler filled with lemonade and water. Don started a fire on his portable grill, and cooked the kebabs to succulent perfection. Seconds after we sat down to eat, a huge swarm of flies appeared out of nowhere, descending on us with a vengeance. These were not pesky little houseflies, mind you, but large, bloodthirsty desert flies. We couldn't decide if they were after our food or us! We ate quickly with one hand and swatted flies with the other.

After gulping down our meal, we packed up and drove up into the high, sloping dunes away from the flies. From our perch atop this enormous sand pile, the four of us watched a herd of several hundred camels crossing the lowlands. We witnessed a touching drama unfold in front of us as a baby camel became separated from its mother. The young camel's soulful cries were disturbing for us to hear, and loud enough for its mother to recognize her offspring calling out, stop in her tracks and turn around. She was at the far side of the herd, headed the wrong way when she heard his cries. Watching that mother and her baby come together in that vast expanse of sand and sky brought tears to my eyes. I could sense her joy at being reunited with her calf.

Off to the left, we caught sight of a lone shepherd and his flock making their way across the lowlands. The tall, lanky, dark-skinned male wore a turban and a flowing robe, just like in biblical times. Carrying only a staff, he used it as a walking stick. Andy and Don wanted to go down and talk to him. Millie-Lynn and I were wearing slacks without abayas and thought our presence might disturb the shepherd, so we stayed in the dunes. We sat, spellbound, taking turns looking through Millie-Lynn's binoculars, as a large ewe in the middle of the flock gave birth to a lamb. The shepherd gave her five minutes to clean up her lamb and get it on its feet before he shouted to get the herd moving again. Andy and Don never did talk with him because he was farther away than he appeared from the dunes. They couldn't reach him before he moved on with his flock. My biggest disappointment of the day was discovering my camera had no film. I had taken perhaps 30 images— all lost—except for those forever saved in my memory.

Chapter 11

King Faisal Foundation

Kathy called to confirm details for dinner the next evening. She said to be at their villa by 6:00. Sean would drive. The event was in honor of Dr. Raymond Lemieux, of Canada, a winner of the 1990 King Faisal Foundation Award in Science. Besides the Lemieuxs, our group included their daughter and son-in-law, four male Saudis from the Faisal Foundation, three couples representing the Canadian Embassy in Riyadh, and the four of us.

We all sat at a large, rectangular table in the Al Khozama Hotel dining room, formally set with hand-scripted place cards, a huge floral centerpiece, candles, crystal, and china. We enjoyed a delicious Arabian gourmet meal of rice, lamb, chicken, yogurt, vegetables, an assortment of sweets and dates, as well as fascinating conversations around the table. Unfortunately, this was the only Faisal Foundation event Andy would be able to attend because of his work schedule, even though he was invited. For me, the evening was but a taste of what was to come in the days ahead.

Next morning, I took a limousine to the Al Khozama Hotel to meet Kathy, the Lemieuxs and a Sudanese representative of the Faisal Foundation. Kathy had arranged for our group to visit Al Marai, a dairy farm located an hour's drive from Riyadh, supposedly the largest dairy farm in the world. Since we were planning on being gone most of the day, I decided to use the restroom at the hotel, one more time. When I reached into my purse for my comb and lipstick, I realized I had forgotten my catheters. For a brief second,

I considered telling Kathy I couldn't go on the tour that day; I was terrified to be away from home without my 'personal supplies'. Up until now, Dr. Judith had been right. Female restrooms in Saudi Arabia were private. Thus, I had become too lackadaisical about making certain I had my supplies in my purse before leaving the villa.

Back in the lobby, I found everyone happily chatting while waiting to board the van. Kathy was talking to several guests, so I didn't want to interrupt her. I decided to go along as planned and try to stay positive. Chances are private female toilets will be available. I kept telling myself I was worrying needlessly.

We boarded a van for the 100-kilometer drive through flat, sandy desert to Al Marai. I sat in the back of the van with Dr. Lemieux, holding pen and notepad as I interviewed him about his background and impressive accomplishments. He told me he had successfully synthesized table sugar in the early 1950s and was currently exploring ways water affects all biological reactions. I felt a special connection to him when he said he had been a postdoctoral fellow at The Ohio State University, my alma mater.

Once we arrived at the dairy farm, the American manager gave us a brief tour of the facilities. I didn't see any signs pointing to restrooms, but I did notice that most, if not all, employees were males. The manager took us into an enormous barn housing 20,000 Holsteins. From there, we went into a spacious milking facility. The manager told us, on average, 35 calves were born, and 9,000 cows produced 220 tons of milk each day. While this fellow managed the farm, a Saudi prince, a son of King Faisal, was the owner. He said the farm currently had 680 employees representing 28 different nationalities, with an average pay equivalent to $78 per month.

After our brief tour, the manager announced lunch was being served inside. He said if anyone needed a restroom, one was available through the double doors leading to the employee dining room. By this time, I needed a restroom like I needed to breathe. I excused myself and went through the double doors. The restroom was a single toilet and sink inside a five-foot tall partition with a foot and a half of open space between the bottom of the partition and the floor. No privacy at all—my worst nightmare. The door to the toilet stood wide open, and there was no lock on the door. Worse yet, this partitioned area was in the corner of a huge dining hall, filled with hundreds of male employees eating lunch.

Dear God, I prayed with all my heart and soul, *please help me, please help me.* Without catheters, I wouldn't be able to relieve myself in this very public place. It would be like telling my ears to bend backward and lay flat to my head. My ears don't work that way, and neither does my personal plumbing system.

I returned to the private dining area where our group was eating. The American manager stood off to the side, overseeing the wait staff. I took a deep breath, walked up next to him and spoke in a low whisper.

"Sir," I said, meekly. "I'm afraid the facilities in the other room will not work for me. I need a private bathroom, and I need it quickly."

My concern was not wetting my pants, an embarrassing inconvenience. My concern was bursting my bladder. We all have angels in our lives, people we remember who did something extraordinary for us that may have seemed insignificant to them but lifesaving for us. Dressed in blue jeans and a plaid flannel shirt, he looked more like a Texas cowboy than the manager of the 'world's largest dairy farm' or an angel. The moment he looked down at me, I saw kindness and compassion in his eyes.

"No problem, ma'am," he said respectfully. "Come this way."

I followed him through the private dining area to a door that led to the outside. We stepped out onto a small, cement-block porch. He pointed to a quaint little cottage at the end of a walkway to the left.

"That's my place. Nobody will bother you there. The front door's unlocked and you can lock it after you get inside if it makes you feel better. The bathroom is on the left past the kitchen. Take your time."

With that, he stepped back in the dining room and closed the door. I hurried down the walkway to his house, went inside, locked the door, found the bathroom. I truly felt Divine Intervention had saved me. I don't know what I would have done if that American manager hadn't been there, nor been as accommodating, nor had a little private house. I didn't even get his name. I went back to the dining room and joined the others at the table without causing anyone to question where I had been or even notice I had been gone. I drank nothing at my meal and was home by mid-afternoon. No more leaving home without my personal supplies.

~

Later that week, seven other winners were welcomed to Riyadh with Saudi hospitality at its finest. Two of the ten winners weren't able to attend for health reasons. My assignment was to meet individually with the six English-speaking winners at the hotel over the next few days. I first met with Dr. Frank Cotton, professor of chemistry and director of the Laboratory for Molecular Structure and Bonding at Texas A&M and Dr. Mohammed El-Saed, co-winners in science with Dr. Lemieux. I later interviewed Dr. Andre Capron, of France, and Dr. Anthony Butterfield of England, co-winners in medicine for their research in schistosomiasis. Their successful collaboration led to the imminent production of a vaccine for this chronic and potentially fatal disease, caused by a parasite infecting freshwater snails, affecting humans largely in tropical Africa and Asia.

While the first five interviews were fascinating, my most memorable interview was with Dr. Khursheed Ahmed, winner in Service to Islam. I was excited to meet this respected leader of a religion I knew little about but was interested in knowing more. As I approached Dr. Ahmed standing next to Kathy in the hotel lobby, I held out my hand to shake his. I realized my mistake right away when he extended his arm halfway to show good faith, but bent back his hand at the wrist to show he could not touch mine. I had momentarily forgotten it was prohibited for a male to touch a female, whether Muslim or non-Muslim. Shaking hands was such an automatic gesture for me as a Western female. I recovered quickly from memory lapse and moved on to more important matters—getting the interview.

Kathy directed us to a quiet area of the lobby where we could talk privately. I began by asking him about his career as chairman of both the Islamic Research Center in Leicester, England, and the International Institute of Islamic Economics in Pakistan. He spoke with passion as he told about what he considered to be his greatest achievement, a conference he organized Mecca in 1976. Held under the auspices of King Abdul Aziz University, the conference was the first time Islamic Economics was introduced to the world as an academic discipline rather than a religious idea.

"Dr. Ahmed, it is truly an honor for me to be able to speak openly with a man of your distinction. I have a question I've wrestled with for years. If you will allow me, it's about religion."

I paused and took a deep breath.

"Please, go ahead," he said.

"I am a Christian and have been all my life. I know Muslims and Jews worship the same God we Christians worship. We share the same history in the Old Testament of the Bible. Why can't we co-exist on this earth peacefully? Why has religion caused so many wars, so many deaths, so much violence, suffering, and ill will among God's people?"

Dr. Ahmed did not appear shocked or surprised by my questions.

"One of the greatest desires of my lifetime has been to help promote a better understanding among the three Abrahamic religions, Judaism, Christianity and Islam," he said. "I deeply believe if Muslims were better Muslims, Jews were better Jews and Christians were better Christians, we would all live in a better, more just and peaceful world."

"I agree completely," I said. "If only it were that easy."

~

The next evening, Crown Prince Abdullah presided over the awards ceremony held at the Al Khozama Center. For the evening's gala event, Prince Abdullah was regally attired in a white ghutra, white thobe and dark-colored royal robe (bisht) with gold trim. He was seated in a large, royal-looking chair in the center of the stage with similarly robed Saudi males on either side of him. I assumed they were all related to the late King Faisal, the Foundation's namesake. The backdrop of the stage was an enormous dark blue banner embroidered with gold Arabic script. The massive flower arrangements placed behind the royals, as well as in front of the stage, added color and elegance to the celebration. The auditorium was filled to capacity, yet females were few in number. Kathy and I sat in the third row on the far right of the auditorium in a segregated area with several winners' wives. The winners themselves sat in the center front row of the auditorium. Other than the English-speaking winners' remarks after receiving their award, the entire program was in Arabic. Fortunately, we had individual earphones for the Arabic to English translation.

Every winner received a certificate containing an abstract of the winning work, a commemorative gold medallion and a cash endowment of SR 350,000 ($93,333) per prize category. In his acceptance speech, Dr. Ahmed made the surprise announcement that he would donate his portion of the cash award to two Islamic foundations, one in Pakistan and one in

England. The audience showed its approval with a hearty round of applause.

After the ceremony, guests attended a formal, five-course dinner. Kathy and I sat at a table with Mrs. Lemieux, their daughter and son-in-law and several other winners' wives. I assumed the evening would end when the dinner was over. We had another outing the next day, a desert picnic lunch at Prince Bandar bin Saud bin Khaled's ranch, and I wanted to be rested for that. As it turned out, another dinner, this time a more private gathering of Faisal Foundation staff, was to be held in yet another room of the Al Khozama Center.

"Kathy, it's almost midnight," I said. "I'm tired and ready to go home."

"This is a once-in-a-lifetime opportunity, Pammy," she whispered. "Relax and enjoy it. You'll never do this again."

Kathy was right. It was a unique and pleasant experience to sit between two charming, attentive, English-speaking, older Saudi males. They took turns explaining each dish of traditional Arabic food including roasted lamb, vegetable dishes, rice, hummus, Arabic bread, dates and whipped butter. The older of the two Saudis served me with his bare hands (a Saudi tradition) and, at my insistence, only a small portion of each offering. At 1:30 a.m. I was stuffed and ready to call it a day. Fortunately, so was Kathy. I was back home by 2:00.

"Good to have you home," my half-comatose husband mumbled as I climbed into bed. "I can't wait to hear about your evening tomorrow."

I wasn't coherent enough to talk three hours later when Andy's alarm went off. I'd tell him about my adventures later. I had to be downtown at the Al Khozama Hotel by 10:30. Within half an hour, our group of about 20 men and women, mostly Faisal Foundation Award winners and their spouses, were off to a picnic at Prince Bandar's desert encampment. Prince Bandar was a grandson of the late King Faisal and a friend of Kathy and Sean's. Kathy said there would be horseback riding and dune buggies for 'entertainment' as if being there wasn't entertaining enough.

After an hour's drive in a luxurious, air-conditioned bus, we arrived at the desert encampment consisting of four, dark-colored, goat-hair tents (two large, two small), a stable for horses, and a corral. We were led into the first tent for a standing-room-only reception. Male Sudanese servers holding incense burners greeted us inside. A personal hygiene station off to the right held a pitcher of warm water, a large bar of fragrant soap and a bowl for hand washing. Another Sudanese server assisted with individual, warmed towels for drying. The tent was decorated with banks of colorful and fragrant floral arrangements and ornate rugs covering the floor. Servants offered us a refreshing glass of fruit juice as we chatted away, enjoying the ambiance of this unforgettable experience with a diverse assortment of guests.

Soon, we were escorted into the second large tent, adjacent to the first. Before us on the carpet-covered floor was a long, white, plastic cloth the length of the tent. I counted four, whole, roasted lambs on huge platters of rice, evenly distributed the length of the cloth, along with numerous bowls of rice, salad, vegetables and Arabic bread. Each guest had his or her own cushion to sit upon. Dr. Butterworth, who sat next to me, counted 42 whole, roasted chickens. Each place was carefully set with fine china, man-sized linen napkins and silverware. The men on either side of me sat cross-legged while I sat with my legs curled to one side completely covered with my skirt.

Bowls of whipped butter and the largest, sweetest, plumpest dates I ever tasted were among the tempting delicacies within reach of every guest. Prince Bander proudly announced that the women in his family had prepared all the food. Everyone applauded as I looked around expecting his wife to appear. Strangely, she wasn't present at the meal, nor did we meet her afterward. I ate as much as I could without being rude or stuffing myself. Fortunately, Saudi food is wholesome, farm fresh and healthy. I remembered what Kathy had said before—that this was a rare treat. I consciously savored the food, the conversation and the sumptuous scene around me.

Afterward, guests wandered outdoors to admire the Prince's stable of Arabian horses. A circular riding area was cordoned off with fencing where we stood and watched as Kathy showed off her equestrian skills by riding a horse bareback. A few brave souls tried out the desert dune buggies. Within an hour or so after our meal, it was time to return to reality. Later that evening, I shared details of my extraordinary day and week with Andy.

"Being with these internationally recognized scholars and upper-class and royal Saudis this week has given me a broader perspective on the cultural diversity in Saudi Arabia," I said. "Up to this time, we've mostly interacted with Saudis at the hospital—some liberal, some conservative, few moderates. The Saudis I've met and listened to these past few weeks seem more moderate. They're all trying to find solutions to problems that could, in time, improve the quality of life for people worldwide; yet, there was not one woman among them. In some ways, it's the same back home. In some ways, it's different."

"How do you mean?" Andy asked.

"The Saudis have different 'classes' of people as we do. Some are educated, some are well traveled and some are not. While we don't regard females as equally we should in the U.S., at least they have a voice. We have laws that guarantee women the right to work, to vote, to hold office, to travel freely, to buy and sell property. Here, married or single males and females don't interact with other males and females or couples in their personal lives. As far as I know, males and females here are segregated in business, education, science and research, even medicine. I wonder if one of the reasons the so-called Golden Age of the Arab culture didn't last past the 12th and 13th centuries was their subjugation of women."

Chapter 12

Ramadan

With my writing for the Faisal Foundation completed, I could focus on the April issue of *The Bulletin*. I wrongly assumed the March issue had been published and distributed two weeks earlier. I learned how mistaken I was when I walked into the office on my first day back.

"Mr. Al Senaidy wants to see you right away," Nabiha said, without her usual welcome-back smile.

When I stepped into his office, Mr. Al Senaidy was holding up a proof of the March cover and pointing vigorously to the upper left-hand corner.

"You're wrong," he said. "I checked with the head of the National Guard."

The text he was pointing to read: *Vol. 2, No. 14, March 1990.*

"Oh," I said, puzzled but amused.

A week earlier, I told him the cover should read *Vol. 2, No. 3* since March was the third issue of the second year of publication. He didn't believe me, nor could he possibly have bothered the head of the National Guard—Prince Abdullah himself—about something so trivial. What he wanted me to know, and took pleasure in telling me, was that I was wrong.

"Besides, Saudis like big numbers, not little numbers," he said, almost as an afterthought.

I was speechless. Mr. Al Senaidy was telling me that my authority, the *Chicago Manual of Style* published by the University of Chicago Press, was invalid. I remembered that I was in the "Magic Kingdom," as Helen tried to warn me when I first arrived. Here, men are the rulers, and they make the rules. I was a woman and a Westerner. Besides, we were in Saudi Arabia, not Chicago. Saudis like big numbers. Anyone with any brains can see that *Vol. 2, No. 14* is more impressive than *Vol. 2, No. 3*.

I wisely chose not to tell Mr. Al Senaidy that if he liked big numbers and didn't mind being wrong himself, it should be *Vol. 2, No. 15* for March and not *Vol. 2, No. 14*. Before I became the English editor, the cover had mysteriously jumped from *Vol. 1, No. 7* to *Vol. 1, No. 9*, from September to October, skipping number 8 entirely. I was fond of Mr. Al Senaidy, but perhaps I had assumed too much about his deeply ingrained views toward all females, Western or not.

Expats notice right away that the male-dominated Saudi society has an insatiable appetite for 'big numbers'. Massive wealth from vast oil reserves made it possible for them to create a state-of-the-art oasis in the last two decades of the 20th century in the middle of the Arabian Desert without financial constraint. I, too, had been dazzled by cutting-edge architecture in their public and private buildings. When we traveled by air, we flew in and out of the magnificent King Khalid International Airport, one of two modern airports in the city. The other airport was an equally magnificent structure outfitted with 24-carat gold bathroom fixtures, among other luxuries, but only for the use of the royal family, numbering in the thousands. In Riyadh, undergoing a massive building boom at the time, the hospitals, educational facilities and palaces were astounding in their size, design, and overall impressiveness. Newcomers soon noticed Saudi preferences for luxury-brand automobiles such as BMW, Rolls Royce, Maserati and Lincoln Continental, and their fondness for 24-carat-gold jewelry—among other indulgences. As much as we Westerners sometimes poked fun at them for their occasional lack of taste and sophistication, their displays of unimaginable wealth were impressive. After all, Westerners had become quite fond of high-end materialism, as well. To their credit, most of the Saudis we knew had extended warm and gracious hospitality to us expats that was endearing. The Saudis only wanted what every other country and culture in the world wants—autonomy, acceptance, recognition, and respect. Nonetheless, we Westerners loved entertaining each other with 'Saudi stories' about their cultural excesses and absurdities. Were we laughing at them or with them? I felt guilty at times for laughing at them because I knew we Americans had laughable traits, as well. It seemed to me that much of our judgment of the Saudis was because of cultural conditioning and perspective; some of it was simple misunderstanding.

At lunch that day, I told an American friend about my brief meeting with Mr. Al Senaidy that morning. She countered with a story of her own about a friend of a friend who observed an upper-class Saudi female trying on eyeglass frames in downtown Riyadh. The Saudi female, accompanied by her husband, lifted her veil to look at herself in a mirror when a mutawa spotted her. The mutawa came rushing toward the couple and ordered the wife to cover her face. Understandably amused by the mutawa's antics, the Pakistani sales clerk didn't have the good sense not to smile until after the mutawa left the store. The mutawa saw him smile, became infuriated and hauled him off to jail. Several days later, the friend of a friend went back to the store to check on the sales clerk. The police detained him until early the next day and made him sign a statement saying he would never smile again.

That evening, I told Andy about being reprimanded by Mr. Al Senaidy and the story about the clerk in the eyeglasses store. Andy told me about a female patient who had come in that day complaining of aches and pains. She was 60 years of age and the fourth wife of a Saudi male. She told Andy 'they'—meaning 'the family'—had 35 children: 10 children with her and 10 with each of two other wives plus five with the fourth and youngest wife. Andy asked if she minded sharing her husband with three other women.

"No," she said. "He quit having sex with me ten years ago which was fine with me."

Each of the four wives had a separate villa within the man's walled compound where they lived happily with all 35 children. Andy then asked why she didn't have three or four husbands.

"You wouldn't know who the father was," she said.

The next day at work, I was in a meeting with Falah, Ahmed and Abdullah to plan for the April issue of *The Bulletin*. We were talking about possible articles when Abdullah suggested an article about the health benefits of wearing a veil. With total seriousness he said veils were good for females because they protected them from eye diseases.

"Interesting," I said. "If veils protect eyes from disease, why don't you guys wear them, too?"

They all chuckled, then Abdullah changed the subject.

~

Toward the end of March, everyone began talking about the upcoming month of Ramadan. It would be my first Ramadan so Andy prepared me for several adjustments I would have to make. Ramadan is the ninth month of the Islamic calendar in which fasting, one of the five pillars of Islam, is observed by all Muslims. Andy said non-Muslims were expected to refrain from eating, smoking, chewing gum or drinking in public or the presence of Muslims from sunup to sundown, even while in an automobile, even on compound. Non-Muslim women were to be sensitive to local customs regarding dress by wearing ankle-length hems, long-sleeved blouses and by covering their hair with a scarf or hijab when requested, which meant if hassled by a mutawa.

An article in *The Bulletin* stated it this way. "While it is good manners to show respect for individual beliefs and traditions, it must be realized that disregard for Ramadan traditions in public behavior is punishable by law."

The article went on to explain that fasting was "total abstinence from food, drink or smoking, sexual intercourse and speaking maliciously about others. Ramadan teaches love, sincerity, and devotion and develops a sound social conscience, patience, unselfishness and will power."

Probably the most frustrating aspect of Ramadan for me was irregular postal delivery. Mail—our main link with the outside world and loved ones back home—was often late, sometimes lost forever. I was horrified by an undocumented account of postal workers setting fire to the backlog of cards, letters, packages and periodicals that had accumulated downtown in the main post office over Ramadan. Apparently, burning it was easier than trying to deliver it all.

Because they weren't allowed to eat from dawn to dusk, Muslims were up most of the night celebrating with their families and then sleeping the rest of the day. Many who worked at the hospital were late for work the next morning or failed to show up at all, although Muslim employees were required to work a minimum of six hours during Ramadan. The first morning of Ramadan when Andy and I walked into the hospital at 7:30, the halls were deserted. The activity level picked up as the day progressed but still, the pace was much slower and remained that way all month. Ramadan seemed similar to Lent for us Christians—a time of abstinence from physical pleasures, fasting and spiritual discipline.

The only significant change I myself had to make at work during Ramadan was getting my morning coffee in the kitchenette on Ward 16 rather than the cafeteria. Normally, the cafeteria offered full-course meals throughout the day, but during Ramadan it was only open from noon to 1:00, offering sandwiches and light salads. I could drink coffee and eat snacks I brought from home in the kitchenette. I would not drink coffee or eat anything in my office if Suhair and Hala were there, out of respect for them. Non-essential activity at the hospital stopped during April since most Muslim employees were gone. I spent my days walking the halls of King Fahad Hospital, writing letters in my office, visiting in the hallways with other non-Muslim employees or on the phone with Kathy.

Halfway through Ramadan, an American friend who had her own car and driver invited me to go with her to a special program at the U.S. Embassy. Finally, I'm going to get away from the hospital for a special outing with my friends to the American Embassy. I was excited about the upcoming adventure although I knew nothing about our speaker other than she was a controversial American author. It turned out she and I had more in common than I could ever have imagined.

Chapter 13

Marianne Alireza

An audible gasp filled the room as American born Marianne Alireza strode to the podium. Smiling and waving, she wore a glittering, shimmering, full-length, red-silk cape trimmed with 24k-gold embroidery. Grasping both sides of the collar, she removed the cape with a flourish to reveal an elegant, full-length red silk gown, studded generously with rubies and emeralds. She waved and smiled at the audience of 200 American female expats who responded by giving her a standing ovation. I, too, couldn't contain my excitement and stood with the others as we cheered and clapped. Beaming with appreciation, she motioned for us to sit and quiet down. She knew very well why we had come to hear her speak. She was one of us, an American woman who followed the man she loved to Saudi Arabia.

"Are you ready for this?", she said in a loud, sultry voice. Once more, the room erupted in laughter, clapping and cheering. Once more, she motioned for us to sit. She had traveled all the way from Sacramento, California, to be with us and we couldn't wait to hear her story.

Marianne moved to Riyadh in 1944 with her baby daughter and her husband, Ali Alireza, the first Saudi national to attend college in the U.S. The two met at the University of California at Berkley in 1941. Everyone wanted to know how she was able to come to Saudi Arabia to live before automobiles, grocery stores, air conditioning and running water. The Arabia

Mrs. Alireza came to was exotic and primitive—a land of sheiks, camel caravans, incense and slaves. She lived in palaces made of mud, while all of us were living in marble villas furnished with air conditioners, telephones, flush toilets you could sit on, washers and dryers.

"It was like living in the Old Testament times," she said. "Camels were the main mode of transportation. There were no medical facilities, no plumbing or electricity. When you got sick, you either got well on your own or you died. It was that simple."

Mrs. Alireza's descriptions of Saudi Arabia in the late 1940s piqued my curiosity, but they didn't hold as much intrigue as the woman herself. What I came to hear was not so much the details of her experience, while interesting, but how she survived the excruciating homesickness, the loss of personal freedom and overwhelming culture shock. I had struggled with all these feelings myself. I wanted to learn all I could from this amazing woman with the hope that it would help me make the most of my remaining months in Saudi Arabia and feel more confident about being here myself.

As someone who has kept a diary for years, I was surprised when Mrs. Alireza confided she never kept a diary in Saudi Arabia.

"I didn't need to write anything down because the events, the people, the emotions are deeply and forever etched in my memory," she said. "As a wound to the flesh leaves a scar, I recall everything that happened to me while living in Saudi Arabia as Ali's wife—the good and the bad—in perfect detail."

Mrs. Alireza said her first meeting with her mother-in-law bonded the two women for life. She described how welcoming it was when Ali's mother greeted her with a warm embrace and told her she loved her, just as she loved her son.

"My first Christmas in Saudi Arabia, my mother-in-law arranged to have a real Christmas tree flown in from Cairo. It was complete with decorations and lighted candles. There were gifts under the tree and a stuffed turkey with all the trimmings for dinner," she said.

"Few in Saudi Arabia had a frame of reference to know who I was or where I came from. You could count on one hand the number of Saudi nationals who knew what was going on in the world beyond the next village. Somehow, Ali's mother knew about Christmas, but she didn't understand it completely. For every other special occasion throughout the year, including my daughter's first birthday, a Christmas tree miraculously appeared in our home, out of nowhere."

Within months of her arrival in the Kingdom, Mrs. Alireza developed a fever she later believed to be strep throat. With no Western doctors to treat her, the women of the harem covered her body with wet compresses while a slave girl fanned her with an ostrich plume.

"It was my own determination, and God's will, that enabled me to survive," she said.

Within hours after she was back on her feet, word came that King Abdul Aziz wanted to meet her. Escorted to the reception room, she waited sitting cross-legged with other veiled women who had been called for the royal visit. Once the King appeared, he made his way around the room greeting each female and sharing a brief conversation in Arabic.

"I was numb from the waist down, unaccustomed to sitting in that position for such a long time, and still weak from my illness," Mrs. Alireza said. "I amused myself by watching as the other women spoke, their veils moving in and out with each puff of breath. I got a giggle fit because it was so humorous to watch—probably a combination of nervous apprehension and disbelief that I was about to meet the King for the first time."

Suddenly, King Abdul Aziz, the legendary hero of Saudi Arabia, stood two feet away. He wore the customary red-and-white checked ghutra and a gold-trimmed black cape over his white thobe.

"He looked larger than life," said Mrs. Alireza. "I rose to my feet with great difficulty on legs that felt strangely detached from my body."

While Mrs. Alireza's college degree was in languages, Arabic wasn't one of them. The only Arabic word she knew, meaning 'hello,' seemed a suitable response to the King's greeting.

"Marhaba," she said, as she turned to walk away.

The Saudi ruler wasn't done with her yet. In a booming voice, the King spoke again and waited for her reply. Mrs. Alireza had no idea what he said, only that he wanted an answer. Frantic to say something—anything—she repeated a word uttered numerous times over her feverish body by the women of the harem.

"Inshallah," she said, to the obvious pleasure of the King, who nodded and disappeared from the room.

Mrs. Alireza was more willing to use a word she didn't know rather than to remain silent, so she repeated the only other Arabic word she could say. When she told her husband of her brief conversation with the King, Ali was greatly amused and proud of his American-born, non-Arabic-speaking wife. The King asked Mrs. Alireza, a Christian, if she would convert to Islam. Her response, meaning 'if God wills it', satisfied the King's curiosity and gained his approval.

Describing the day her husband's brother telephoned to inform her that Ali had divorced her and taken another wife, Mrs. Alireza became emotional for the first and only time during her talk. Although she didn't reveal when Ali divorced her, where she was at the time, or what she was doing, she said her first fear was for their five children. They were all older than seven years of age and in school in Switzerland. Saudi law gives the husband full custody of children older than seven. Mrs. Alireza said details of the divorce and ensuing conflicts over custody are revealed in her book, *At the Drop of a Veil*. Her husband had the book banned from the Kingdom before his death in the late 1970s. Eventually, she was reunited with her children. Prior to his death, she and Ali worked out an amicable visitation schedule. When they grew to adulthood, all of the children chose to live in Saudi Arabia. Mrs. Alireza never remarried, and she never became a Muslim. Only her close relationship with King Faisal, assassinated in July of 1958, made it possible for her to enter the Kingdom to visit her grown children. News of her arrival in Riyadh for her appearance at the American Embassy never made local newspapers. If the mutawa had learned of her visit, there would have been trouble, even though the Embassy was off limits to them.

Following her talk, I walked up to the podium to shake her hand. I felt a kinship with this woman who was a Christian, and who came to Saudi Arabia because she loved her husband. Once here, in spite of the losses, hardships, and adjustments, she learned acceptance and forgiveness, lessons I was still in the process of learning.

"If you could distill all you learned by firsthand experience in Saudi Arabia, what would your best advice?" I asked.

"You get out of life what you put into it," she said. "No matter what happens to you, life goes on. When I was a child growing up in Oklahoma, nobody traveled or knew what was going on in the world. I feel fortunate to have learned through firsthand experience. Knowledge and understanding lead to wisdom. We need more wisdom in our world today."

Her words captivated me. I was seeing and hearing a real-life example of the kind of person I wanted to be. Her heart had been broken, and her family separated physically, yet they had remained close in spirit. She learned to forgive her husband and by doing so gained more than she lost.

She became a better citizen of the world.

"Only Ali divorced me. My Arabian family didn't divorce me. We proved that even if you come from worlds apart, you can still have mutual love, respect, and tolerance. The compensation for the disappointments has been the people I have grown to love and who love me. They have made all the difference."

Marianne Alireza's words inspired me to see my time in Saudi Arabia and my absence from my boys' lives from a more positive perspective. My intentions to remain optimistic would be tested again and again in the months ahead.

~

The day after Ramadan ended was the first day of Eid-Al-Fitr, a five-day 'Feast of Breaking the Fast' celebrated by Muslims worldwide. Andy and I were invited to a festive Eid-Al-Fitr open house at Amina and Asiru's attended mostly by their Nigerian friends. Amina wore a stunning ankle-length dress made of colorful Nigerian fabric, with a matching head covering. She served fried chicken and fried rice with a curry sauce and miniature orange and carrot cupcakes. Ayesha, Tahira and Farida wore fancy party dresses as the family greeted a steady stream of guests arriving throughout the afternoon.

Because of Ramadan, *The Bulletin* wasn't published in May, so I began working on the June issue. I was delighted when Mr. Al Senaidy gave me my two assignments: the lead article on nursing, and a profile on Dr. Judith, my physician at King Fahad. I was thrilled because I already knew Dr. Judith, and also because hers would be the first profile of a female physician ever to appear in *The Bulletin*.

I sat with rapt attention as she told about her life in Saudi Arabia as a female physician, as the wife of a neurosurgeon at King Fahad, and as the mother of two adult children. Dr. Judith's advice only confirmed what Marianne Alireza had shared with me a few weeks earlier.

"Growing up in Australia, people had the notion that anyone who was different was not desirable," she said. "Today, I know from my own experience that people are much the same all over the world. Prejudice and hostility are a result of fear of other people you don't know. Living in Saudi Arabia is a lesson in getting on together. Instead of saying, 'How peculiar,' you say, 'How interesting.'"

When I asked if she treated only female patients, Judith smiled and shook her head.

"One of my first patients was an elderly Bedouin man who came in with some ailment," she said. "As different as he and I were in age, looks, culture and religion, we hit it off right away. I was so impressed with that."

When I asked for her most remarkable experience as a physician in Saudi Arabia, she told me about another male patient, a general in the Saudi Arabian National Guard. After listening to his complaints about chronic constipation, she told him it was not a medical problem but a behavior problem.

"His diet was lacking in bulk and fiber. I prescribed a kilo of prunes every day and told him to come back in a month. When he returned, he was elated. He said he was 'cured'—a changed man. He had been a captive of his inability to have a daily bowel movement that controlled his life. In fact, he ordered a supply of prunes for all the soldiers in the fields."

While the first part of Judith's story was amusing, the second part of her story was astounding.

"The general told me he planned to host a gala dinner in my honor at his palace. I could invite my husband and as many guests as I wanted. Andrew and I, our son Peter, and good friends, Jean and Ramsey, were chauffeured by limousine to the general's palace in Rawdah, an exclusive area of Riyadh."

Once they arrived, male servants escorted the men through one door of the palace. Female servants escorted Dr. Judith and Jean through another entrance that led to the harem—the female quarters.

"We were served tea, cookies and dates as we conversed with the women of the harem, including two of the general's wives who spoke little English. Thank goodness Jean and I could speak some Arabic. For three and a half hours, we sat looking at party dresses modeled for us by the younger females. We ate dates and cookies and drank multiple cups of tea, all the time wondering where our husbands were and when we were going to be able to join them and leave."

Finally, a male servant summoned Judith and Jean into the dining room, now empty of male guests. Several female servants handed them plates and motioned for them to help themselves to leftovers from the meal served earlier to the men.

"After Jean and I finished eating alone in the empty dining room, the general appeared to thank me once again and to say goodnight. He told me he had announced to the prominent guests gathered at dinner that he was eternally indebted to me because I had cured him of a lifelong ailment. Our husbands and my son joined us and the limousine came and took us home."

Judith was amused rather than offended by the cultural differences that kept her away from the banquet in her honor.

~

In early May, shortly before our trip to Greece, we learned that Latvia officially declared itself an independent nation. Latvia was annexed by the Union of Soviet Socialist Republics (USSR) against the will of the Latvian people in 1940, three years before Andy was born in Riga, the capital. Andy's parents were elated with the news, and while we were happy for them, we couldn't imagine the depth of their feelings. Andy was a small boy when neighbors alerted the family the Russian police were looking for Andy's father so they could send him to Siberia. His father took off in one direction so his family could flee in another direction. Andy has no memory of his escape as a two-year-old on foot with his mother, grandmother and brother Ray, 3. After some months, his father found the family in Czechoslovakia. They all made their way back to Germany where they lived in displaced-persons camps until 1949, when they came to the United States. We were indebted to Andy's parents for all their help enabling Andy to work in Saudi Arabia for several years. His dad handled all our financial affairs from Grand Haven and both his parents looked after Peter, who spent his summers with them.

  While we enjoyed our brief stay in Athens for Andy's rheumatology meeting, we were most excited about our trip home in June. I flew to Grand Rapids where I rented a car and drove to Petoskey for Bob's graduation from Petoskey High School. Andy flew directly to Tallahassee for Leis's graduation from Leon High School in Tallahassee. I couldn't have been more proud of my son Bob as he walked down the aisle of Bay View Auditorium to be handed his high school diploma. A few days later, all of us, including John, Bob, Peter, Leis and Andy and I were in Grand Haven for Andy's parents' 50th wedding anniversary celebration at St. Patrick's Catholic Church.

  The day after we returned to Riyadh following our two-week trip home was the first day of hajj. Able-bodied Muslims from around the world were making their way to Mecca in Saudi Arabia. Thus, the pace at the hospital would slow once again, especially now that Mr. Al Senaidy was on leave to the U.S. for three months. No explanation was given for his departure or for the length of his absence. Salah would be in charge.

Adding to my frustrations at work was my slower-than-usual re-entry adjustment after our June trip home. Saying goodbye to the boys and my family never got easier; in fact, it became more difficult each time. So much was going on in their lives that I was missing—a sadness that never went away. My heart and mind were in two different places. I was torn between two concepts of 'home'. I cared deeply about what was happening in everyone's life back in the U.S. I also cared deeply about my day-to-day life with Andy in Saudi Arabia. I tried to consciously savor this special time together. After all, we'd be going home in six months, *inshallah*.

Chapter 14

Emmanuel

On my first day back at work, I was sad to learn that Emmanuel, our Public Affairs photographer, was a patient in King Fahad Hospital. My heart sank when Nabiha told me he had a malignant brain tumor. Surgery to remove the tumor had not been successful. We all loved Emmanuel—a quiet yet friendly man, a hard worker, a talented photographer and always punctual. He was married, the father of five children in Nigeria. He was also a Christian.

By the time I found out about Emmanuel's illness, doctors had done all they could to get him strong enough to go home. He wanted so badly to see his family before he died, but that was not to be. As a Christian, I had to go to Emmanuel and offer whatever support I could. Nabiha said Emmanuel was frightened and depressed about dying. King Fahad Hospital had no official Christian pastors on staff to support him in his faith. It was up to each of us, as Christians, to do what we felt moved to do, discretely, in our own way, on our own time, to help him.

When I walked into his private room, I sat in the chair next to his bed. I waited to see if he was awake. His eyes were closed and he was breathing heavily. His head was wrapped in bandages. He was propped up on pillows and his hands were clasped together on his chest as if praying.

"Emmanuel," I whispered, not wanting to startle or awaken him. Slowly he opened his eyes, looked at me and smiled. He was weak and lethargic, but I could tell he was happy to see me. I nodded and smiled at him and then decided to share some thoughts with him about death and dying from my perspective.

"Emmanuel, I brought my Bible to work today, but you're the only one who knows this." He smiled, closed his eyes and nodded.

"I've never been in your situation so I can't say I know how you feel. I know my heart is breaking for you, and I know I would want somebody to affirm my faith for me and with me if I were you."

Witnessing my faith to others was not something I had much practice with or felt comfortable doing. I had never read from the Bible to a dying person. Even though as a child I attended Sunday School faithfully for years and learned all about Jesus and His life, death and resurrection, I was not taught to voice aloud what I believed and why.

I began reading at verse 1, Chapter 5 of St. Matthew in the New Testament and read through verse 18, the Beatitudes from the Sermon on the Mount. This passage had always been a favorite of mine. I was hoping it would comfort Emmanuel, too. I stopped reading, saw Emmanuel was weeping, and I reached for his hand.

"It's okay," he said. "I always loved the Beatitudes. May I ask a question?"

"Yes, of course."

"Do you believe I'll go to heaven when I die and that Jesus will watch over my family after I'm gone?"

"Yes, I do, Emmanuel. In Sunday school, I was taught that your name 'Emmanuel' means 'God with us.' Your name and your baptism assure you that He is with you and your family—always. I also believe what the Bible says about life after death, and that death only takes the body. Your spirit or soul is eternal. I believe Jesus will come for you at the time of your death, and you will know He is here. He is here with you now, with us, right now, today. After we die, because of Jesus Christ, our soul lives forever with God and in the hearts and memories of those we loved and who loved us."

I had not planned to say what I said, and I worried I had said too much. Emmanuel closed his eyes again. I waited a few moments, trying to decide if I should leave or stay. I decided to say goodbye and come again the next day.

"Emmanuel," I said softly, "I'm leaving now. I'll be back again tomorrow. I want you to know I'll write to your wife and family and tell them how much we love and respect you in Public Affairs. I'll also tell them I came to visit you and that you're not alone here—that your Christian friends are looking after you and praying for you. I'll tell them your faith is strong and that you're being brave and courageous in spite of your illness."

When I came the next day, the nurse told me Emmanuel had slipped into a coma. The doctors prescribed a sedative after he complained of pain. I visited Emmanuel two more times, but only to stand by his bed and say a prayer for him and his family. We never spoke again, but the last time I visited him, I noticed the worry lines across his forehead and around his mouth had disappeared. Emmanuel looked peaceful and ready to go. He died the following day.

My time with Emmanuel opened my eyes to a new awareness of how strong my faith was even though I had never expressed my beliefs so openly before. Growing up, we always prayed before meals and bedtime, yet my parents never spoke about what they believed and why. I couldn't recall hearing them talk about their doubts and fears regarding faith, or asking us if we had questions about theological matters. Emmanuel gave me a greater gift than I had given him by being the strong and faithful Christian he was, even at a time when he was frightened, suffering physically, and missing his family and home.

A few days later, we learned of another troubling death. Our good friend, Don, a Canadian, Harvard-trained neurologist Andy considered to be one of King Fahad Hospital's best physicians, had a female patient, a Saudi, who died unexpectedly. An investigation into her death eventually exonerated Don of any negligence, but that didn't satisfy the family. They appealed to Prince Abdullah who placed Don under house arrest and pulled his passport 'until further notice'. Don and Millie-Lynn were scheduled to take a three-week trip, a two-week holiday in Europe with friends and one week of a medical symposium in the U.S. All of it was delayed 'indefinitely'.

Eventually, they were able to reschedule their two-week holiday with friends, but Don missed his symposium. The entire incident left us all feeling uneasy. The laws of justice and retribution in Saudi Arabia seemed tribal and mysterious. I knew we were at their mercy should anything happen to one of Andy's patients. While all this was going on with Don and Millie-Lynn, Andy had six days of general medicine duty meaning he was 'on-call' 24/7 for anything that came into the Emergency Department—*anything*. He would be responsible for all patient care he provided regardless of whether their ailment or condition fell into his area of expertise. To say this put me on edge is an understatement. As always, it seemed when my spirits were down, something would distract me and cause me to shift my focus. This time it was a candid interview with a Saudi national named Salah, the manager of Media Services. Unlike my colleague in Public Affairs, this Salah was more progressive and more Western in his worldview.

"Our worst problem in Saudi Arabia is how males regard females as second-class citizens," he said. "Change will come, but it will come slowly. Until those who hold to the more traditional views die off and are replaced by people with more modern views, we will live in a male-dominated society."

As refreshing as Salah's comments were to me, no way could I incorporate them into the article I was writing about the history of the hospital. A more traditional point of view appeared a few days later in the *Saudi Gazette*.

Muslim Women Are Free!
Muslim women who are proud of their Islamic identity and who dress modestly and behave in a dignified way and do not indulge in dancing, drinking and pre-marital sex are usually regarded by non-Muslims as 'backward', 'enslaved' or 'downtrodden'. But when Western women behave like prostitutes, dress shamelessly, enter beauty competitions, expose their bodies to promote merchandise, drink alcohol in bars with men and do the go-go dance like monkeys, they are regarded as 'liberal', 'progressive' and 'equal'. Islam is the only faith that is really a blessing to women. It has come to truly liberate women from the shackles of evil, degradation, prostitution and slavery. Islam wants women to concentrate on the all important role of wife, mother, home-builder and educationist. That is why the Prophet (Peace Be Upon Him) said: Paradise lies at the feet of mothers. Today, in Western and non-Muslim societies women are regarded as mere chattels to be used, abused and discarded like plastic dolls. Women are still regarded as humans without a soul and are accused, like Eve was, for all evil and the downfall of Adam and man in general.

What surprised me about this article was, while much of it seemed exaggerated and judgmental, some of it made sense. As a Christian, I was taught to be modest in 'thought, word, and deed' as well as in my dress. I was also taught to respect myself and my body, and not to abuse alcohol. What I was observing in Saudi Arabia was how different we were from the Muslims yet how similar. Why then did we come to regard each other with such animosity and suspicion? Could it simply be a matter of misinterpretation and miscommunication?

Something else happened at the hospital that gave me pause—as well as an excuse to spend time in the nursery. Helen stuck her head in my office door to tell me a Saudi VIP had given birth to twins—a boy and a girl—and she wouldn't have anything to do with them. Helen was short staffed and needed help feeding and rocking the babies. It seemed the father, who was 15 years older than his wife, had taken a second wife while the pregnant wife was waiting to go into labor with the twins. With three young children of her own at home, the mother of the twins was depressed and refused to see or hold the babies.

Suhair and I gladly volunteered to help as needed. After the nurses bathed and fed the babies their bottles and burped them, we rocked them to sleep with great pleasure . . . for only five days. The sixth morning when I arrived, the mother and babies had left—without explanation. We knew nothing of where they had gone or why. Even Helen was tight-lipped.

A labor and delivery nurse told Suhair and me it was common for Saudi mothers to care little about seeing their babies after birth. They had given birth so many times it was no longer an occasion for joy. One exception the nurse told us about was a Saudi mother who was blind and couldn't wait to 'see' her baby.

"I've never seen a new mother check her baby over so tenderly, so thoroughly and lovingly as that mother," the nurse said. "She touched her baby girl all over, her head, her face, her arms, legs, hands, body, and feet. She counted her fingers and toes, smiling and making happy 'oooh' sounds the entire time. We were all impressed watching her. We couldn't help thinking if every baby came into the world greeted by such love and adoration, what a wonderful world this would be."

Andy's contract with Witikar gave us a generous holiday allowance: 30 paid vacation days and one week of paid medical education leave per year. We finally decided to take a trip in September to the Far East—Hong Kong, Bangkok, and Singapore. In October, we would spend two weeks in the U.S. for Andy's American College of Rheumatology meeting in Seattle. We would leave a week early so we could visit our families in Michigan and Ohio—all four of our children and our parents. Besides Leis's visit in a few weeks, we had much to look forward to, and we were excited.

Leis was originally scheduled to arrive the middle of July. Because of a mix-up with her visitor's visa at our end, her visit would be abbreviated, and she would arrive the end of July. She had to be back home in time to unpack and repack for her freshman year at Michigan State. It took Andy a while to straighten out legalities with the American Embassy before rescheduling her plane ticket. As it turned out, she came on July 27th, so we had a week in Riyadh before she, Andy and I would fly to Abha on a three-day holiday.

When she arrived, Leis found two kitties living in our villa. Our temporary feline guests, Lucy, the mother, and Brownie, Lucy's daughter, were finicky Persian cats. Leis had more patience with them than I did. They belonged to Andy's colleague, a rheumatologist from Egypt, and his family. The family was going back home for a visit, so Andy volunteered to board their cats for three weeks.

We asked our Canadian neighbors to feed Lucy and Brownie for a few days while we were in Abha. Brownie picked fights with Lucy, although Lucy was sometimes the perpetrator, too. They couldn't eat out of the same dish without hissing at each other and getting into a tussle. For some reason, I had misgivings about leaving the cats, or did I have misgivings about other fights brewing close to home? Perhaps it was a discussion I overheard the day before at the hospital between two physicians, a Canadian and a Pakistani, about oil quotas and squabbles between our next-door neighbors, Iraq and Kuwait. Thinking about their conversation made me feel uneasy, like something ominous was about to happen.

Chapter 15

The Invasion

The morning sun provided a welcome warm-up as we waited outside our hotel in the brisk mountain air. A road-weary limousine pulled up to the front entrance precisely at 8:00 a.m. Our Middle-Eastern driver wore a threadbare wool jacket over a white thobe with no ghutra indicating he was non-Saudi. He tossed our bags in the trunk, climbed behind the wheel, and off we went down the winding road in a cloud of dust and sand.

        Andy, Leis and I had just spent a relaxing weekend near the city of Abha in Asir, the mountainous western region of Saudi Arabia overlooking the Red Sea. Cut off from the rest of the world for two blissful days, we spent our days hiking in the hills surrounding our hotel and strolling through local markets. At night, we dined on succulent and perfectly seasoned lamb shish kebabs and my favorite Arabic desserts, baklava and cinnamon date cake in the hotel dining room.

        My light-hearted holiday mood began to fade when I noticed our driver's strange behavior. Sitting forward in his seat with a firm grip on the steering wheel, he would speed up, slow down, and then speed up again. He was chewing a miswak[18], nervously shifting it from side to side in his mouth. His gaze darted back and forth from the road to the rearview mirror, eying all three of us in the backseat. I placed my hand on Andy's leg and grasped his

---

[18] A twig from the arak tree used by Bedouins for cleaning teeth.

knee with such force that he looked at me with alarm. I rolled my eyes in the direction of the driver, just as the man spoke up.

"You ... Americans?"

"Yes," Andy said, pulling himself closer to the front seat to better hear what he had to say. "Why?"

"Big trouble in Kuwait. What you think? Iraq? Kuwait?"

"What big trouble?" Andy said.

My throat tightened. My heart leaped in my chest. I felt a wave of nausea.

"Iraq took Kuwait in the night. They killing people. They taking over Kuwait."

"Oh, my God," I gasped, as goose bumps covered my arms.

The rumors I had heard at the swimming pool were true. I *just knew* it was more than social swagger when I overheard two physicians talking about a military showdown between Iraq and Kuwait over oil quotas. One of the docs had connections to the royal family who told him big trouble was brewing. Listening to their casual banter about something so serious unnerved me. When I mentioned it to Andy, he said a showdown was unlikely, so I tried to put it out of my mind, except I couldn't. After all, we were in the volatile Middle East.

"What time did this take place?" Andy asked the driver.

The driver shrugged his shoulders, and took his hands off the steering wheel. He lifted up his open palms to indicate he didn't know or didn't understand Andy's question.

From that moment on, our mid-life adventure in Saudi Arabia became a mid-life crisis for me. With my heart pounding and my hands trembling, my mind went into overdrive, attempting to process what this unwelcome news might mean for us, for our safety, for me ever seeing my boys again. Granted, we knew nothing other than what this fellow had just told us. We heard nothing at the hotel that morning when we ate breakfast in the dining room and said goodbye to the concierge. My rational mind told me our driver may have his facts wrong. My gut told me our driver was right. All I could think about was how much I didn't want to die in Saudi Arabia. I had come here 14 months earlier with reservations but not because I thought I might die here. I wasn't ready to die yet, but when it happened, I wanted to be closer to home. I knew if I started to cry I wouldn't be able to stop. Instead, I prayed. *Please, dear God, keep us safe and help me stay sane and sensible until we get back to our villa where I can cry in private.* I didn't want my emotions to frighten Leis, embarrass Andy, or distract our driver who was already driving way too fast to suit me.

We made it safely to the nearby airport in what seemed an eternity. The driver lifted the bags out of the trunk more carefully this time and bowed respectfully to Andy after Andy gave him a tip.

"Have a nice day," the driver said casually, like it was something Western expats liked to hear rather than because he knew what it meant.

There's no tourism in Saudi Arabia, other than fair-skinned expats like us traveling within the Kingdom. That morning, it appeared we were the only expats at the airport. Worse than that, Leis and I were the only females. A dozen or so bare-chested workmen with loosely wrapped rags on their heads stared blankly at Leis and me as they sat on their haunches lined up in front of the airport in the hot sun. As much as I hated wearing my abaya, I was glad to be covered in one. I wasn't veiled or wearing a headscarf, but I could understand why a woman in this culture might want to at times.

Andy led the way as we dutifully followed behind him through the small airport crowded with staring males. We made it through check-in and then to our gate, keeping our gaze low to the ground. We boarded our commuter plane arriving back in Riyadh in less than an hour. Once inside our villa, we dropped our bags in the foyer and bounded upstairs. Andy flipped on the television expecting to see and hear a live broadcast with details of the invasion. Nothing appeared on any of the channels other than the usual daytime programming. What did we expect, knowing mutawa and the government controlled all the TV, radio and print media? Still, we had reason to believe the small country of Kuwait, less than a four-hour drive to the east of us, was under military attack.

"Call Schaefer," I told Andy. "It's unbelievable this could be going on without anybody here knowing about it."

Andy's friend Jack Schaefer confirmed our fears. The invasion had occurred 36 hours earlier, approximately 530 kilometers from Riyadh, yet there was no public confirmation of the event—no newspapers, no television reports, no local radio coverage. It was apparent the Saudi government ordered a news blackout to prevent widespread alarm. We tuned into the BBC (British Broadcasting Company) on our broadband radio and listened to sketchy but deeply disturbing details of the invasion. Nobody knew what was going on in Kuwait, except for reports of murder and mayhem.

We were able to get an open line to call Andy's parents and my mother to tell them we made it back from Abha, and we were okay. Mother said she'd call the boys, and Andy's parents would let his side of the family know we were safe.

I had made arrangements with Mr. Al Senaidy for Leis to assist me at the hospital, without pay. That way, we could spend more time together during her visit, and Leis would get to know some of our friends and colleagues who worked there.

Everything appeared normal Sunday morning as we drove from our villa down to the hospital. People went about their business, walking along sidewalks, riding buses and bicycles, driving cars. All I could think about was the chaos unfolding just three hundred miles away. Kuwaiti men, women, and children were being taken from their homes, brutally tortured or killed by gunfire or bayonets in front of their families.

Reaction among the hospital staff was mixed. Some were nervous; others said it would blow over. Optimists believed Saddam Hussein would retreat when the Americans threatened military force, but, of course, he didn't. After a few days of wishful thinking, a larger conflict appeared imminent.

On Wednesday, August 8, 1990, I typed a letter to Mother, trying to sound upbeat even though I was worried about how quickly news reports were changing:

Dear Mother: Within a few hours of hearing something or writing it down in a letter to you, it becomes passé. We listened to the BBC at breakfast and learned that U.S. troops and planes are winging their way to Saudi Arabia. Though I must admit the news sent a chill down my back, I want to assure you we are in absolutely no danger. My anxiety is for the innocent Kuwaiti people who are in much more danger than we are. We are in a military hospital complex in Riyadh, so whatever military activity takes place will be east of us. We are well protected and well supplied. Our hospital has its own water supply and electrical generator. There are many qualified and competent people here with us—Americans, Canadians, Brits, and Europeans— so we are in good company. The worst that could happen is we would become a field hospital for casualties, in which case we would not be able to leave until the crisis was over. The Saudis could not possibly run this compound and hospital without expatriates, and no one with any integrity would pull out now.

At the end of my letter, in the postscript, I told Mother we had just received word that the Riyadh airport would close temporarily because U.S. planes would soon be landing. As I walked back to my office after mailing Mother's letter at the hospital post office, I felt an urge to call her. Sometimes open lines from the hospital were more predictable than from the villas. It was 4:00 p.m. in Riyadh so it was 9:00 a.m. in Worthington. Mother answered on the first ring.

"Pammy! I'm so glad to hear your voice! How are you?"

"Glad to hear your voice, too, Mother. I'm fine, but I'm also scared. Everyone here who has any authority or experience is telling us we're safe. One minute I want to leave; the next minute I think we should stay."

"What does Andy think?"

"Andy thinks it's exciting. He says there's not going to be a war and Saddam Hussein is bluffing."

"What about Leis?"

"She thinks it's exciting, too. I'm not sure she and Andy realize how serious this could be. Time will tell, but for now, we're fine."

"Take care of yourself, Pammy. Make every day count."

I could hear tears in Mother's voice, but she would never pressure me to come home. *Make every day count.* Four simple words uttered by my mother calmed me. I wrote Mother's quote in my journal so I could be reminded of it in the days and weeks to come. Throughout my childhood, rather than lecturing us, Mother exhibited emotional strength, pragmatic creativity and clear thinking, no matter the circumstances. By example, she gave me the strength to stay grounded in faith from half a world away.

After dinner that evening, Andy, Leis and I sat in the dining room as I told them about my phone call with Mother. The phone rang upstairs in the family room. Andy ran to answer it and then yelled down to us.

"Schaefer says to go to the roof."

Out of breath from climbing the three flights of marble stairs two steps at a time, I quit breathing altogether when I looked up at the early evening sky. From the northeast, countless olive-colored U.S. military transport planes were heading toward King Fahad International Airport. Andy squinted against the setting sun's last rays to get a better look at the huge planes parading overhead.

"What are they?" I shouted over the loud, steady drone coming from the sky over our villa.

"C-5s carrying troops and tanks."

Andy gets goose bumps when he's emotional. His arms were covered with them. The overpowering sound of their engines made it difficult to talk. In silence, we watched these large, U.S. cargo planes heading west in a straight line. I couldn't see where the parade ended, there were so many. All I could think about was John and Bob and how I didn't want to die in Saudi Arabia. My knees began shaking. A multitude of goose bumps covered my arms. I couldn't look any longer; I had to go inside.

Early next morning, Bob called.

"Time to come home, Mother," he said.

Bob was only 18, but he sounded so grown-up, more like a worried father than a worried son. While I was touched by his concern, I felt guilty for giving him and John cause to worry.

"We'll be fine, Bobby," I said, trying to sound confident. "We have plans to go to the Far East in September and then to the U.S. in October. Andy said if things don't settle down before then, we'll come straight home from Singapore rather than fly back to Riyadh."

At this point, nobody knew for sure what was going on although some were predicting gloom and doom. For me, lack of verifiable information was torture. My untamed monkey mind imagined the worst with every rumor I heard.

Before we went to bed that night, Andy turned on the BBC. The latest news from Baghdad was discouraging. Saddam Hussein was calling for a Holy War and the overthrow of the Saudi government. I had my first of several sleepless nights that night.

At 7:30 the next morning, my spirits were lifted to see our Canadian friend Don walk into the hospital. Millie-Lynn decided to stay back in Canada for a while. They had been away for Don's medical conference.

"It never occurred to me not to come back," he said when I asked if he was worried about the situation. "Millie-Lynn wasn't keen on coming back, but said she will as long as there's no war."

What a morale boost to see Don looking and acting so confident and chipper when others we knew were leaving. It was good to see some enthusiasm about coming into the hospital instead of going out.

That afternoon, Andy and I were walking down the main hallway of the hospital when we bumped into a Palestinian pediatrician. Andy knew him from the Iskan Clinic, the outpatient family practice clinic affiliated with the hospital, located off compound a mile or so north. Their exchange began friendly enough until this fellow made a remark about the American intervention that didn't set well with Andy.

"You sound like Saddam Hussein," Andy said.

"Muezzins all over Riyadh are denouncing Americans for interfering," this fellow countered as he stepped closer to Andy, staring at him angrily as if he was about to grab my husband by the collar.

"All you Americans are looking for trouble and, believe me, you're going to get it."

I reached for Andy's sleeve and pulled him away before he could respond verbally or get into a fistfight. I didn't let go until I had a chance to glance backward to see the Palestinian doctor striding briskly in the opposite direction, the sides of his open lab coat flapping behind him. I told my dear husband as clearly and discretely as I could that from now on, he should keep his opinions to himself. The only time he could speak his mind was at home when we were alone.

With each passing day, the mood in the hospital shifted from shock to anger, and then from denial to fear. Leis and I noticed a change in Nabiha. Friendly before, she seemed detached and aloof. Before the American military presence, Nabiha was a good friend. Now, because our country was perceived to be threatening the stability of the Muslim culture in Saudi Arabia, she would hardly speak to us. I don't know what I would have done without Suhair, who told me not to take Nabiha's behavior personally. Many Middle Easterners shared the same feelings Nabiha had toward Americans. Suhair and I could talk about anything without getting upset with each other. We were able to express without judgment all these strange feelings and emotions we were both having. The American military presence, while giving Americans a greater sense of security, heightened a feeling of paranoia and distrust among the Saudis as well as Sunni and Shia Muslims[19] from other countries. Since my arrival, I proudly wore a lapel pin of side-by-side, miniature American and Saudi flags on my photo ID. That night, sadly, I took the pin off and put it away. I remembered my dad's warning many years ago: "Don't go looking for trouble." Good advice at any age, especially now. Everyone's nerves were on edge, including mine. I didn't want to say or do anything to enflame touchy feelings with anyone.

On Sunday, August 12, a reporter from *The Muskegon Chronicle*

---

[19] The differences between Sunni and Shia Muslims initially stemmed not from spiritual differences, but political ones. Today, the differences are more complicated. Saudi Arabia is predominantly Sunni with a minority of Shia Muslims.

phoned us at our villa. Although he didn't say, I assumed he knew we were in Saudi Arabia because of Andy's parents who lived in Grand Haven, not far from Muskegon. He first spoke with Andy and asked if we planned to come home because of the situation in Kuwait.

"Here in Riyadh, things are quiet," Andy said, downplaying the drama going on behind the scenes. "We're a long way from the trouble in Kuwait. With American forces now in place, I feel much better. At first, we were all afraid of chemical warfare. Now that's unlikely."

The reporter then asked to speak with me.

"What makes you nervous about what's happening?" he said.

"Lack of accurate information," I said, in contrast to Andy's more cavalier answer. "Some expats are hysterical and leaving however they can. I heard 200 nurses have left Riyadh already. Before the invasion, we had a staff of 120 physicians and 600 nurses. Now we only have 400 nurses. I've only heard of one physician who's left, a Pakistani, and that's because his wife is pregnant and wanted to go home to have her baby. Some of the nurses and technicians I know are leaving with a carry-on and the clothes on their backs. They arrange for an exit visa claiming an emergency at home, or to go on holiday, and never come back."

The reporter also spoke with Andy's father in Grand Haven and asked him what he thought of the situation in the Gulf.

"It's shaky," Dad was quoted as saying. "We know what war means. The younger generation is brave, but we have experience from the old country."

Dad's words were chilling. He and Andy's mother had first-hand experience as refugees in Europe during World War II. After fleeing the Russians who forcefully took over their home and property in Latvia, they lived in displaced-persons (DP) camps in Germany for five years. Andy and his brothers Ray and George were too young to remember the experiences their parents endured by the grace of God. I was sensitive to Mom and Dad's concerns because I knew they lived through the dangers and uncertainties of military conflict. War wasn't a joke or an exciting adventure. World War II was brutal, and they were reliving their fearful memories because of us.

Articles that included quotes from Andy and me regarding the invasion of Kuwait also appeared in *The Petoskey News Review*, *The Grand Rapids Press*, and the *Grand Haven Tribune*.

Two days after our telephone interview, I received a call in my office from an American who worked in Information Technology at King Fahad Hospital. I was flabbergasted when Michael told me Andy and I were celebrities back home because of an article in *The Grand Rapids Press*.

"Oh, my goodness," I said. "How .. er ... interesting."

Michael went on to say a female employee of *The Grand Rapids Press* knew Andy's relative, John Sinkevics, a reporter there. John then contacted Andy's father in Grand Haven. Michael was in contact with this woman through telephone lines in such a way that he could get written messages back and forth in real time, like a phone call, only faster, with words on paper. He said if I wanted to get a message to my family, I could type out a message on his computer that he would then transmit to *The Grand Rapids Press*. His contact there would duplicate the message, make copies and mail it to whomever we wanted. Once more, my father was right when he told me not to do anything I didn't want to read about on the front page of *The Worthington News*, my hometown newspaper. Amazing how quickly word got around, even from halfway around the world.

The next day, I made an appointment to go to Michael's office, the only second-floor office in the hospital, located up a flight of stairs above the executive offices. I felt self-conscious as I walked through the executive offices carrying a sheet of paper with my message on it, hoping nobody would stop me to ask where I was going and why. When I got upstairs, Michael let me type the following message into his computer:

Dearest Families: We have found a new, state-of-the-art way to communicate. This brief message to you, to assure you we are okay, is being sent over telephone wires, via computer modem, from Riyadh to Grand Rapids. The kind lady on the receiving end is willing to print three copies and distribute them to Grand Haven, Worthington and Hillsdale. This is cheaper than phone calls and much quicker than conventional mail, even when we send letters and packages with friends coming to the U.S. I don't know how often we'll send these "computer messages" because we don't want to take advantage of our kind friends at the terminals, but perhaps once a week or when there's an urgent message. We'll be sending letters with Leis when she flies home on August 22nd. So much is happening here that I'm not sure I can cram it all into one letter. Most assuredly, we are fine and confident we will continue to be. We will stay in close touch with you as much as possible.

We didn't know at the time that this "new, state-of-the-art way to communicate" was our first exposure to e-mail. Cell phones weren't in wide use, either. If they were, we didn't know anyone who had one in Saudi Arabia. While we didn't send many computer messages, knowing the technology was available gave me comfort. I had another sleepless night after reading an internal memo Michael gave me, obviously written by an expat.

At a senior staff meeting today, the subject of a rumor came up that several employees gave telephone interviews to North American press. Managers were told to remind employees that this is against all rules, both company and government. In fact, all employees working in Saudi Arabia sign a non-disclosure agreement in which we promise not to tell ANYONE what it is REALLY like over here in the Magic Kingdom.

While I couldn't remember if I ever signed such a statement, I knew I was lucky this time. My mother always told me to keep my eyes and ears open and my mouth shut. Funny how my parents' mantras had stood the test of time and were helping me cope all these years later during an unsettling time in my life.

Chapter 16

A Daring Adventure

Presumably to quell concerns about impending war, everyone living and/or working on the compound was invited to a party on the MC Plaza. The evening would begin with a buffet dinner followed by traditional Saudi music and dancing, games and prizes.

    Early afternoon the day of the party, I was in our villa waiting for my sister to call at 1:30 from Worthington. I picked up the phone on the first ring at 1:31 p.m. The connection was excellent—a rarity—and Marcia sounded upbeat. With 10,000 U.S. expats living in Riyadh, concerned friends and relatives back home were frantic to hear how the Gulf crisis was affecting our daily lives. Many of our American friends had received calls from hysterical relatives pleading with them to come home. It was good to know my sister wasn't one of them.

    "There's a recent Ohio State University School of Journalism graduate from Columbus broadcasting 'live' from Riyadh on WBNS-TV," Marcia said. "Her name is Juli Klyce and she's staying at the Marriott in Riyadh. She escaped across the desert from Kuwait and had a harrowing experience."

    I could hardly grasp what Marcia was saying. At this point, the mass exodus from Kuwait into Saudi Arabia had begun. The government had set up temporary emergency tents east of Riyadh to accommodate some of the fleeing Kuwaitis. Other Kuwaitis were staying with relatives in Riyadh. The government was also preparing more permanent housing downtown for hundreds of refugees, perhaps even thousands. It seemed unbelievable that an OSU graduate could be among them and staying in a Riyadh hotel after escaping from Kuwait nine days after the invasion.

The minute Marcia and I finished our conversation, I dialed the Marriott, doubtful the young lady would be there. I was delighted when I asked for Juli Klyce and the concierge replied in perfect English, "One moment, please."

I could hear the room telephone ringing, but no one answered. Encouraged by the fact that the man I spoke with seemed to know Juli Klyce was, indeed, a guest there, I hung up and waited ten minutes before dialing again. Still, no answer, but this time, he offered to page her over the hotel's loudspeaker system. When she didn't respond, I asked the man if I could leave a message and my phone number.

Ten minutes later, the telephone rang—it was Juli! I couldn't talk fast enough to tell her why I was calling. Connecting with someone from home I didn't know, yet with whom I had so much in common under such unusual circumstances, was exhilarating.

"Hi, Juli, I'm Pam Daugavietis and I live in Riyadh. Until I was 25, I lived in Worthington, Ohio. My husband and I work at King Fahad Hospital, and I graduated from The Ohio State University School of Journalism in 1965. My first job out of college was at WBNS-TV!"

My verbal autobiography took less than 15 seconds to deliver. I could feel my heart thump, thump, thumping inside my chest as I waited for Juli to respond to my rapid-fire monologue.

"Oh," she said, "How wonderful to hear from you."

Her subdued demeanor surprised me, considering what she had been through. She sounded so young, so confident; I was twice her age and not nearly as self-assured. I couldn't imagine myself being so calm, cool and collected after such a daring adventure.

"How did you manage to get out alive?" I asked.

Speaking calmly and distinctly, Juli, 23, related details of her escape across the desert. She disguised herself as a man and eluded Iraqi soldiers at the border before setting off with a male colleague, without food or water, across the desert to Riyadh. I knew I had to meet this young woman who graduated from my alma mater 25 years after I did, and who was now in the same strange part of the world so far from home.

"Juli, can you come to King Fahad Hospital this evening for dinner and afterward a party with traditional Saudi music and dancing? My husband and I and our daughter can pick you up at 4:00 this afternoon. We'll have time to talk before dinner."

"Oh, I'd love to," she said. "I hope this isn't a problem, but I have to place a secure telephone call to WBNS-TV in Columbus at 6:00 p.m. Riyadh time to give them a 'live' report."

"No problem," I said. "You can call from our private phone here at the villa and then we'll all go to the dinner."

An hour and a half later, our car turned into the entrance to the Riyadh Marriott. I spotted a tall, slim, attractive young woman wearing sunglasses waiting by the front entrance of the hotel. She wore a tan, loose-fitting blouse, an ankle-length skirt the color of butterscotch, and low-heeled sandals. She carried a small tan purse over her shoulder but no briefcase. The moment I spotted her I jumped out of the car and ran over to greet her.

"Juli?" I asked, extending my hand.

"Yes," she answered, reaching out for mine.

"I'm Pam," I gushed and giggled with joy as I vigorously shook her hand with both of mine. "It's so great to meet you!"

"Thank you, Pam. It's nice of you to invite me for dinner."

Juli's shoulder-length, auburn hair was pulled back in a ponytail. She wore no jewelry and little make-up. Her attractive appearance and relaxed demeanor amazed me. I was expecting a battle-hardened war correspondent. Instead, she made me think of Brenda Starr, a popular comic book character from the 1950s—gutsy and glamorous. I liked her immediately. I introduced Juli to Andy and Leis as she climbed into the backseat. On our drive back to the compound, she began telling us her captivating saga.

"Right after I graduated from Ohio State in June of 1990, I came to Kuwait under the auspices of the National Council on U.S.-Arab relations. I worked as a reporter for an English-language newspaper in Kuwait City. The invasion took them completely by surprise.

"Of course, we were aware of the growing tensions between Iraq and Kuwait over oil quotas, but we never feared an invasion. Although Iraqi troops seized the airport and radio and television stations right away, international phone lines stayed open. Thankfully, I was able to talk to my family and my contacts in Washington, D.C. Knowing it might be days before I and other Americans could leave Kuwait, they asked me to keep a journal. For a while, I was a link between Kuwait and the Western world.

"At first, I stayed in my office. I could make calls to my parents, and I even did an interview on National Public Radio."

"Did you have electricity and running water?" Andy asked.

"No, but we survived."

"Did you have food?" I asked.

"Enough to keep us going."

"Were you scared?" Leis asked.

"Not especially at first, but as the days went on, I became more and more concerned about getting out safely. We heard some fairly grizzly reports about how Iraqi soldiers were treating Kuwaiti citizens."

Nine days after the invasion, Juli managed to flee during the night from her office to her apartment. From there, she planned her escape three days later with the help of an Iraqi colleague who had also worked at the newspaper. Not all Iraqis were supportive of their brutal and erratic ruler.

"We joined a caravan of Kuwaiti nationals on a four-hour drive across the desert to Saudi Arabia. I wore a thobe, covered my head with a ghutra, and wore sunglasses. I have never been so scared, or so hot, in my life," she said.

"Our caravan consisted of fifteen cars and my friend was driving a Mazda 929, not exactly a desert car. I shook with fear but kept looking forward, not allowing myself to think about not making it. The most obvious danger was the Iraqi Army, now behind us, but the desert can be a relentless enemy, as well."

Four times during the escape Iraqi soldiers forced them to turn around. They had to double back across the open desert to avoid the roadblock. Getting stuck in the sand or having a flat tire can be fatal disasters in the desert.

Sadly, I could personally testify to this grim reality. I saw anxious mothers waiting outside our Emergency Department holding severely dehydrated babies connected to IV drips while waiting their turn for additional care. Some of the grieving mothers held deceased babies. Iraqi soldiers took away their food and water and ordered civilians to leave the country. Although numbers were unknown, some elderly adults and young children were said to have died of dehydration after their vehicles stalled in the rough desert terrain.

In the early morning of August 12, at the exact time Juli and her companion were crossing the desert in Saudi Arabia, her mother was in Hilton Head, S.C., suffering from severe anxiety. Telephone lines were cut almost immediately after the invasion, so Juli had had no contact with her family for ten days. Her mother later told her that a peaceful feeling came over her at the exact time Juli was safe in Riyadh. She knew, intuitively, that Juli was fine, even without knowing details of her daughter's daring escape.

By the time Juli, Andy, Leis and I returned to our compound, it was almost time for Juli to call the TV station in Columbus. Juli asked if I would be willing to say a few words during her report about what it was like living in Riyadh, and whether we would leave.

"Yes, of course," I said, momentarily forgetting about the warning I had received several days earlier.

I couldn't resist the temptation to surprise my mother and sister by being on their local TV station where I had once worked. After dialing the compound operator for an outside line, it felt like a miracle when I heard my mother's phone ringing two seconds later. Many times before we had tried to call home and had to wait for a line or give up completely. No answer. The operator came back on the line. I asked him to try another number. This time I gave him my sister's number.

"Hello," Marcia answered from her kitchen in Worthington.

"Marcia, it's Pam," I said, knowing she would be more than a little surprised to hear from me a second time that day.

"WHAT ARE YOU CALLING FOR AGAIN," she shrieked, twenty decibels higher than before, fearing an emergency at my end.

"I'm going to be on WBNS-TV, live, in about fifteen minutes with Juli Klyce. I called Mother and she wasn't home. Please record the program, if you can."

The interview went well, although I wondered later if, once more, I had been too forthcoming. The reporter asked me how expats at King Fahad Hospital were reacting to the invasion. I told him many nurses and other support staff were in the process of leaving or had left. Witikar said those employees leaving after August 27th would have to pay their own way home. When the reporter asked if Andy and I were staying, I said we were because we felt our presence was important to others who had elected to stay beyond the August 27th deadline. All this was true but not what an American expat public relations staff member should be saying to an American TV station with a national affiliation. I never heard any repercussions about what I divulged during the interview that day, but I sometimes worried Andy might get in trouble for having such a talkative wife!

As we drove Juli back to the Marriott that evening, she and I discovered we had even more in common. Both of us were not only Ohio State grads, but also Worthington High School grads. She and her mother had lived in the same area of Worthington where my widowed mother still lived. When we pulled in front of the hotel, I asked her how long she planned to stay in Riyadh.

"If the saber rattling quiets down, I'd love to stay, but my visitor's visa expires soon," she said. "I'm pursuing a job possibility in the United Arab Emirates with the National Council on U.S.-Arab Relations. Without a job, I have no reason to be here. If that doesn't work out, I'll go home."

The night before Leis went back to Florida, we invited Juli to go with us for shawarmas and fruit drinks. She was delighted because as a single woman without an igama, she didn't get out much. She reported that the job in The United Arab Emirates fell through, and she still didn't know where she would go or what she would do next.

Later that evening, we said goodbye in front of the Marriott where we first met a few weeks earlier. Juli gave us each a quick hug and said she'd stay in touch by telephone to keep us informed of her plans. She waved as she disappeared into the hotel.

As sad as I was to see Juli leave, our goodbye with Leis the next evening was more difficult. It seemed we were always saying goodbye to someone. At least we knew we'd see Leis again, and she'd always be in our lives. We both would miss having her around. She said she wasn't worried about us, but she admitted she would be relieved when January came, and we could come home. She was also a bit anxious about beginning her freshman year at Michigan State. Andy and I assured her she would do fine and that Grandma and Grandpa would look after her until we got home in January.

"Growing up and going off to new places, new responsibilities and new challenges isn't easy but it's inevitable and necessary for a full and rewarding adult life," Andy told her. "We're proud of you, Leis, and we know you'll do fine."

Our feline boarders would be going home soon, too. While it had been fun at times to have them around, especially with Leis there, they required extra attention because of their unpredictability. We worried that one of them might get out the door and disappear into the desert. Both of them still had their claws, and were as close to being feral cats as any so-called domesticated cat we had ever known. When their owner came for them, it was a happy day, and a huge relief, for both of us.

Chapter 17

Ahmed's Wedding

Several days after Leis left to go back to school, I passed Mel in the hallway. He seemed distracted and unusually grim. Before the invasion, he was always easygoing and smiled all the time.

"Mel, what's wrong?"

"War coming. I worry about getting paid. I worry about not getting home. My family, in Philippines; they worry, too. Can't talk. Gotta go."

I smiled, shrugged, and waved him off with a sympathetic look.

On my way to Public Affairs, I crossed paths with two friends coming down the hall, both Egyptian nurses. Avila had her arm around Samia who appeared to be crying. They stopped and looked at me with sorrowful eyes.

"What's wrong?" I asked, although I knew.

"We have a strong faith in God, but we are fearful," said Avila.

"Nobody knows what's going to happen. Only God," said Samia. "We must be strong, but what about our families?"

Words were inadequate. All I could do was reach out and give them each a hug. Only two weeks after the invasion and already many of my hospital friends were panicking.

On my way to the mailroom, I nearly collided with Mamiz, my Kurdish friend, rushing out of the lab. I reached out to stop her and held her by her shoulders while she sobbed.

"Mamiz, what's the matter? What happened?"

"I can't leave. My husband can't leave. If we do, our supervisor at the lab just told me we'll lose our jobs. My daughters, so small. Only two and ten. I don't want them here. What if we all get killed? They have to go to London. To my sister's. Administration won't let me go. My Filipina maid has to go instead. They all three terrified to go without me."

What could I possibly say to her to help her feel better? All I could do was hold her while she shook and cried. By the time Mamiz and I hugged goodbye, I was crying and shaking, too. I couldn't get the image of her tear-stained face out of my mind. When I got back to my office, Suhair was waiting for me. I dreaded telling her Andy and I had decided to leave January 10th, the day Andy's contract ended. The U.S. military build-up was the tipping point for me. It was time to go, more my idea than his.

Suhair grabbed my hands and squeezed them tightly. "Pam, you can't leave. You mustn't. Not now. Please reconsider."

"Suhair, we have to leave. I'm so sorry. I don't know what to say. Like you, my heart is breaking. I will miss you terribly."

She let go of my hands and stepped back, taking in a deep breath. She looked at me with sympathetic eyes.

"I would do the same if I were in your shoes," she said.

When I met Andy that night to drive home, he narrowed his eyes at me. "What's wrong? What happened today?"

"All my friends at the hospital are panicking . . . for good reason," I said. "Many fear they won't get paid. They're afraid they won't get home—ever. Just hearing their stories devastates me. War is coming. I've lost confidence in a peaceful resolution to all these conflicts over oil. I told Suhair we were leaving in January. She begged me to stay."

"No doubt there's uncertainty right now," Andy said. "But panicking won't help. Perhaps there's something to be learned by witnessing this."

"I resent all the talk about how it's such a big adventure to be here now," I said, casting a disapproving look at my husband. At times, his opinions about the present situation seemed too cavalier.

"Thank goodness you're not egotistical like some of the expat doctors and executives I've overheard talking. These guys have made plenty of money here, no doubt invested safely back home, with a lot less to lose than workers from countries with no political clout, people like Mamiz, Suhair, Mel and Tav. Every day another country issues a travel advisory, all except the United States, of course."

Tears welled up in my eyes. Andy glanced over at me to see if I was joking or serious.

"Today in the cafeteria, everyone had a gas mask clipped to their belt. The entire conversation was about 'when' we get gassed, not if. All of them are from countries that have issued travel advisories. There I sit with no gas mask, trying to eat my lunch. It's absurd. I know how you feel, but I want to go home. And I won't leave without you."

As soon as we were in the door, Andy told me to go upstairs and try to relax while he started dinner. I climbed the stairs shaking with fear and trying to compose myself. As I gazed eastward out the window in our second-floor family room, my thoughts shifted to what was going on back home. *What are the boys doing right now? Are they worried about me? I don't want to die here. Will I ever see them or my family again?*

Andy came upstairs, put his arms around me and held tight. He gave me his handkerchief to dry my tears. He took me by the hand and led me to the couch where we sat down, facing each other.

"Pam, if you want to leave now, we'll leave." I looked at him with a hint of a smile. I knew he meant what he said.

"Pam, I had no idea you felt this way. I didn't realize how scared you were. I would never put you through this intentionally. I'm truly sorry."

"I've been trying so hard to be supportive of your desire to stay that my fears broke through today," I said. "They had to come out sometime. Seeing all my friends at the hospital so upset and crying and worried about their families is heartbreaking to them, and to me. I feel guilty because I know I can leave if I want to and they can't. It's such an awful feeling. I don't want to be a coward, but I don't want to die here, either."

"You're not going to die here; you can trust me on that. If you want to go home, we'll go home. I won't let you go alone, and I won't force you to stay or make you feel guilty because you don't want to. I can begin tomorrow to make arrangements for us to leave. We could be home in a matter of weeks."

"What about the money? Would you get paid?"

"I don't know, but that's not as important as your peace of mind."

Next morning, I felt I had awoken from a bad dream. I knew Andy would go with me if I wanted to leave, which was a huge relief.

Later that day at the hospital, Ahmed came walking down the hallway, grinning from ear to ear, and handed me a fancy looking envelope.

"You and Andy *must* attend my wedding," he said. "No excuses."

I opened the over-sized invitation, in Arabic, printed on shiny, pearl-white stationery.

"Ahmed, you know I can't read this. When is your wedding and where is it?"

"Thursday, August 30th, 8:00 p.m., Suliamania Wedding Palace, four blocks east of the Al Khozama Hotel, two blocks from the Panda grocery store. I'll print out a map for you."

"Andy will find it. He knows this city fairly well," I said, wondering why we received the invitation at such a late date. The wedding was only four days away.

"Congratulations, Ahmed. I am so happy for you and . . ."

"Monira."

"Monira is one lucky young woman."

"Don't forget to bring your invitation to get in the door, and veils are optional," he said with a smile.

At the same time Ahmed was planning his wedding, Falah was risking his life to find his brother-in-law who had stayed behind in Kuwait to fight Iraqi soldiers. A few days after the invasion, Falah drove alone to Kuwait City to rescue his sister and her nine children. All ten of them moved in with Falah and his wife and three children. Falah said his sister cried all the time for her husband and Falah couldn't stand it any longer, so he went back to Kuwait with a buddy to see if they could find the brother-in-law. Such selfless courage was amazing to me, especially since Falah was such a quiet, mild-mannered, slightly built man who never raised his voice or showed anger or ill will toward anyone. Sadly, Falah's second attempt to find his brother-in-law was unsuccessful. He and his buddy returned to Riyadh alone.

Each day at work brought more heart-wrenching stories like Falah's but also stories that made me smile. Several nurses told us at lunch one day about what they had witnessed at Olaya Mall, a favorite shopping destination for Saudis and expats alike.

"Now that the U.S. military is here, male and female soldiers are out and about doing what everyone else does on their days off—go shopping," the one nurse said. "The mutawa have been given strict orders not to hassle female soldiers. Watching these females out in public wearing long pants or desert shorts without abayas drives mutawa crazy. Instead, mutawa weren't hassling American female soldiers, they were hassling Saudi males for looking at female soldiers; they were confiscating their igamas and hauling them off to the mosque to pray."

My contract with Public Affairs was up for renewal. While they offered me another one-year contract, I declined because it was now certain we would leave January 10th. Instead, Salah said they would pay me 20SR an hour as a 'casual hire'. I could work when I wanted to up until the time we left in January. We still didn't know if our trips to the Far East and Seattle would work out. If they did, being away wouldn't affect my status in Public Affairs. What was surprising was the positive first-year review I received from Salah. Now that he had taken over the department in Mr. Al Senaidy's absence, his attitude toward me had changed. He wrote in my review that I was "presentable, punctual and productive" and that I was "reliable and trustworthy" and "full of initiative and enthusiasm." It made me wonder if he was the same man I knew months earlier, or if it was something else. Perhaps it had to do with his relationship with Mr. Al Senaidy, and how being in charge made him more appreciative of the staff's efforts. Whatever it was, I was grateful to be able to continue working.

Even though it was only August and January was months away, expats planning to leave before the end of December told us to get our belongings shipped home as soon as possible. In the event that we had to evacuate sooner, we would be forced to leave all the treasures behind that we acquired during our stay. We would live out of two suitcases between now and January and the walls of our villa would be bare once again. Andy and I decided we'd rather be safe than sorry, so we drove to the outskirts of downtown to Camel, Inc., a local shipping company, to make arrangements. While there, we loaded our trunk with packing boxes.

What we didn't know was that we had to alert security to inspect our packed boxes before they were sealed and as they were being loaded into the truck. Housekeeping wanted to make sure we weren't shipping home our villa's furniture and household goods, as if we would even want them. On the day of the scheduled pick-up, since we hadn't alerted security, they wouldn't let the Camel people in the front gate. When Camel didn't show up, we phoned the company. They said it would be at least a month before they could reschedule another pick-up.

Juli Klyce called to say she was leaving the next day. She said she would miss talking with me and thanked us again for our hospitality. I would miss her, too. Having her a phone call away in Riyadh was a comfort, another connection with home. She said her mother wanted her to leave Saudi Arabia and get a job somewhere in Europe, anywhere but the Middle East.

"Take care, you guys, and get out of here before something terrible happens," she said before she left. I never saw or spoke with her again.

~

The night of Ahmed's wedding finally arrived. Helen, an Australian nurse named Michelle, and I were the only female hospital staff to attend. Andy was on-call, so we drove alone in case Andy was paged to go to the hospital. Helen and Michelle took a limousine. The map Ahmed gave us was accurate, so we had no trouble finding the Suliamania Wedding Palace. In fact, we spotted it a block away because of pulsating lights strung all over it, top to bottom. The parking lot was full of cars. A line of guests stood outside the double doors waiting to get inside. Some males wore business suits like Andy's; some wore traditional Saudi thobes and ghutras. All females wore abayas and hijabs; most of them wore veils.

As we entered, males were directed to the right, females to the left. Andy and I agreed to meet back at the front door at 10:55 p.m. unless he received an earlier page. If so, he would send someone to find me because I felt safer to ride home with him rather than take a limo with Helen and Michelle. We were surprised to discover the event was a reception only. The wedding ceremony was a private legal exchange held earlier in the day that involved signing papers and Ahmed handing over the dowry to Monira's parents, a Saudi custom.

Helen and Michelle were waiting for me inside the female entrance. A Filipina maid ushered the three of us down a hallway into a huge auditorium-like hall. Enormous crystal chandeliers cast tiny rotating lights everywhere. Ahmed's sister, the only other English-speaking member of his family, greeted us warmly. Ahmed's mother, three younger sisters and sister-in-law shook our hands and smiled when Ahmed's sister introduced us. She told us her mother, sister and sister-in-law had chosen Monira to be Ahmed's wife and made all the wedding arrangements. We smiled and nodded in acknowledgment of their success since the Suliamania Wedding Palace was filled to capacity. I quickly counted eight rows of three sections each, with 20 seats per section. As far as I could see, all 480 seats were taken. The sizable seats were luxuriously upholstered in deep maroon leather, with plenty of open space between sections and rows. From back to front, the floor sloped toward the stage, with a large, flat area between the first row and the stage.

Ahmed's female family members, like all the other Saudi females in attendance, had shed their black abayas, headscarves and veils to reveal colorful, high-style attire accentuated by dazzling gold jewelry. As I looked across the hall, I saw a sea of elaborately coiffed, happy, dark-haired females of all ages. Some of these guests were standing in front of their seats, some were mingling row to row, throughout the theatre-like hall. All of them were talking, laughing, hugging and air kissing. Many had fancy, lace-like henna designs on their faces, hands and ankles in black or cordovan-colored tan. Most of the dresses appeared to be one-of-a-kind, designer dresses, some beyond description. One young woman wore a dress that resembled a tossed salad. Layers of stiffly starched panels of transparent fabric in every imaginable shade of green, trimmed with glitter and sequins, stuck out in every direction from her shoulders to her ankles. Every time I caught sight of her she was standing. I suspected it was because her dress made sitting impossible.

African female servants wearing turbans and full-length sarongs in colorful fabric carried trays filled with tiny cups of tea and crystal goblets filled with ice water back and forth in the rows of guests. More female servants followed with trays of cookies, dates and other tempting sweets. Still others carried incense burners so guests could waft exotic-smelling fumes of burning sandalwood through their hair and on their hands, arms and loose garments. Helen, Michelle and I sat together toward the back of the auditorium, mesmerized by the show surrounding us.

Soon, a six-member, female drum group began gathering on stage and setting up their instruments. A lone female vocalist sat in a chair off to the right of the stage behind the drummers and began warming up her voice, humming and then singing softly into a hand microphone. At first, the drumbeat was difficult to hear above all the chattering, but the chatter died down as the music grew louder, faster and more vigorous. Some of the females shouted out occasionally as the vocalist sang. Gradually, the atmosphere grew more festive as young females from the audience went up on stage and began to dance erotically, not together but alone, moving their torsos, hips and arms to the drumbeat. Older females in the audience started clapping as they watched the show underway on stage. Dancing was to attract the attention and approval of mothers and sisters looking for a wife for their son and brothers. I was disappointed when I looked at my watch and saw it was time to leave. I bid goodbye to Helen and Michelle. Andy was waiting for me by the front door, guarded by two hefty male guards.

"What was your evening like?" I asked.

"So much food—plentiful lamb, chicken and all kinds of strange side dishes. It was a free-for-all buffet rather than a formal, sit-down dinner. I saw Ahmed and spoke with him for a few minutes, but we had no entertainment."

"Amazing. Absolutely amazing," I said as I described to Andy everything I had witnessed that evening. At the hospital the next morning, I couldn't wait to ask Helen what happened after I left.

"You hadn't been gone five minutes when a servant came to tell us Ahmed wanted us to meet Monira," she said. "We put on our abayas and followed the servant to a room upstairs where Ahmed and Monira were waiting to be presented to the females downstairs."

"How sweet," I said. "Wish I could have met her, too."

"We told Ahmed you and Andy had to leave because he was on call. Ahmed was nervous and sweating profusely. He was wearing a black tuxedo and Monira was dressed in a long, white, Western-style bridal gown. She was heavily made up and wore bright red lipstick. What fingernails she had left were painted red, too. Her long black, curly hair was pulled back from her face. She was slim, pretty and oh, so young."

"Does she speak English?" I asked. "Did you talk with her?"

"No, she doesn't speak English, but she smiled shyly when Ahmed introduced us."

Helen and Michelle went back downstairs just as the drumming, singing and dancing were winding down.

"All of a sudden, the drums started up again with a soft, steady beat," Helen said. "The roomful of women made a high-pitched trilling sound with their tongues as they pulled on their hijabs, abayas and veils. We put on our abayas, too. Ahmed and Monira entered through the back door, walking arm in arm down the aisle to the front of the auditorium."

Helen said the room grew quiet. Ahmed and Monira smiled nervously at the audience, then sat in two middle chairs of a row of chairs placed at the front of the room. A photographer took several photos of the couple alone. Monira then pulled out a black veil and put it on since it was unlawful for Ahmed's father to see Monira's face. Helen said it was quite a contrast to her white bridal dress.

"Ahmed's father, three brothers and three younger unveiled sisters entered the auditorium," she said. "The three sisters sat on either side of Ahmed and Monira. Ahmed's father and three brothers stood behind Ahmed, Monira and the three sisters for a group photo. Ahmed's mother declined to be in the photograph."

Helen said the father, brothers and newlyweds then left the room. Helen and Michelle decided to leave, too. They were tired and ready to go home. A dinner of leftovers from the men's earlier meal wasn't reason enough to stay. Besides, they had been eating sweets and drinking tea all night, so they weren't hungry. Ahmed and Monira would take a three-week honeymoon in Europe.

Andy and I decided we would go to Hong Kong in two weeks if peace prevailed in the Gulf. If war broke out and we went home instead, I wouldn't see Ahmed again. I pondered the possibility I wouldn't see any of my Saudi friends again. Being torn between wanting to leave and not wanting to leave was unsettling. At least now I knew if I wanted to leave badly enough, Andy and I would go together.

Chapter 18

Impending War

With only two weeks before our scheduled departure for the Far East, and no new developments in Iraq and Kuwait, we started getting excited about our trip. For a month after the invasion, I resisted even thinking about a holiday. Assuming we wouldn't be able to go, I put it out of my mind. Our only question at this point was whether Andy would get approval to attend the American College of Rheumatology meeting in Seattle. My fear was that Administration would learn we were leaving in January and not let us leave again in October, one week after returning from Asia. Living with so much uncertainty was unsettling.

Sadly, our friends Carol and Martin would soon leave permanently. Amina and Asiru said they would stay because Nigeria wasn't stable, and Saudi Arabia was better for them financially. I was comforted to know Amina would be here, but I was sad for her. I knew how much she wanted to take the girls and go home.

On Saturday morning, I attended another coffee at the American Embassy for women living in Saudi Arabia. I met a woman named Jane who moved with her husband to Saudi Arabia from Iran in December of 1978, three weeks before the Shah went into exile. She said her husband had been with Boeing Middle East Limited his entire career, and was now head of their Middle East operation. Earlier, the couple had lived in China where he was with Boeing, and together they helped to establish China's first chapter of the Red Cross.

I told her I came to Riyadh with my husband who was a physician at King Fahad Hospital. I said I was a writer in the hospital's Public Affairs Department.

"Would you be willing to help me write my memoir?" she said. "I'll pay whatever you ask because we've had so many adventures I want to write down and preserve—for our children and grandchildren."

"Gee, I don't know," I said, taken aback by her request. "My husband and I are planning a trip to the Far East next week. If all goes well, we're planning a trip to the U.S. a week after that. We won't be back in Riyadh until the first week of November. I'm not sure there's time for me to help you with such a large project by the time we leave for home in January."

"Would you be willing to meet with me privately? Perhaps you'll change your mind when you hear my story."

We agreed to meet the next afternoon at my place. I called security to let her in the front gate. At 1:00 p.m. sharp, a black Lincoln Continental limousine with darkened windows pulled in front of our villa. I watched from the upstairs window as the uniformed driver got out on his side. He walked around to the other side of the limo, opened the back door for Jane, then stood at attention, in the hot sun.

"Your driver is welcome to come inside," I said when I greeted her at the front door. "I'm sure it would be more comfortable than waiting outside."

"Oh, no," Jane said. "He can wait there. I don't trust anyone, not even my driver."

She paused, squinting her eyes and peering around the living room, eying the ceiling from corner to corner, "are you quite sure your home is secure?"

"Secure? You mean from being wire-tapped?"

"Yes."

Coming Home to Myself ~ Page 197

"Good heavens," I said. "I never thought about our villa being 'bugged.' What makes you think it might be?"

Jane proceeded to tell me about their lives in China and Iran as I took notes. She said they left Iran eleven years earlier, just weeks before the overthrow of the Shah and the return of the Ayatollah Khomeini.

Leaning toward me, Jane lowered her voice.

"Today, in Riyadh, with so many Saudis upset with the American presence and the threat of war, the mood is the same as it was right before the Shah was forced to leave. We were lucky to get out when we did. It was a scary and unstable time. I learned to trust no one."

That was all I needed to hear.

"Jane, as much as I would like to help you, I can't," I said as I put down my pen and closed my notebook. "I've never written anyone's memoir so I can't say I'm experienced. Besides, I don't want to do anything that might cause trouble for my husband before January. I hope you can understand. I've never been in a situation like this; quite frankly, I'm scared. All I care about at this point is getting home alive."

Jane graciously accepted my refusal to help and said she understood my concerns. She and I never connected again.

Several days before we left for Hong Kong, Carol, Amina and I went shopping together, one last time. They had been my shopping buddies and best friends in MCX for over a year. I knew I would stay in touch with them after we parted ways, but I doubted if all three of us would ever have the opportunity to shop together again.

We went to Batha on the shopping bus. When it was time to go home, we returned to the covered bus stop where we were dropped off. We waited in the shade and watched traffic whiz by in all directions. We were startled to hear a male voice shouting in Arabic. The voice grew louder and louder and then stopped. Not five feet away was an open vehicle carrying a wild-eyed mutawa staring at us with a scowl on his face. He was shouting at us through a bullhorn. Amina, who understood Arabic, said he was ordering all Muslims to go quickly to a mosque to pray since it was almost time for the noon prayer. He had a long, bushy beard and was wearing sandals and a knee-length, white garment that looked like a man's nightshirt. He climbed out of the vehicle, took a few steps toward Amina and began screaming at her through the bullhorn, pointing to her head and shaking his finger. He was so angry, the veins on his neck stuck out. Amina's was covered, so she didn't know why he was so angry. The mutawa then pointed to her legs. The blue jeans she was wearing were not acceptable.

"*Woman,*" he yelled again, in English, "*Cover your legs.*"

Amina fumbled with her packages as she tried to pull the sides of her abaya together around her legs. The mutawa then moved to Carol, who wore an abaya but not a hijab. Her curly blond hair caught his attention.

"*Cover your hair, woman,*" he yelled.

Carol's face turned red, not from embarrassment but unexpressed anger. All three of us had heard stories about non-compliant females being taken to jail for similar offenses, an adventure we didn't care to experience firsthand.

"I don't have a scarf," Carol said as assertively as she could.

"*I said cover your head, woman—immediately.*"

I dropped my packages to help Carol pull her abaya up over her head, trying not to pull it up too far in the back to expose her bum. He then started wagging his finger at me but before he could yell, I had pulled my abaya up to cover my hair, trying to look as compliant as I could. Finally, the mutawa and his driver continued on their way, leaving us fuming and sputtering about how silly all this was, especially Amina, a devout Muslim.

"*That is not Islam,*" she said vehemently.

Several Filipinas, also waiting for the bus, inched closer to us for protection. Clutching their abayas tightly around their shaking bodies, they looked up at us with fearful eyes and whimpered softly. As annoying as the episode was, the three of us decided our brush with the mutawa might have been a beneficial experience. In future years when tempted to look back wistfully on our 'halcyon days' in Riyadh, we would remember not all of them were blissful. Besides, the experience gave us renewed compassion for females in Saudi Arabia, and elsewhere around the world, faced with humiliating treatment on a daily basis.

~

Our trip to Hong Kong, and Singapore gave us something to think about besides the precarious situation in Kuwait. Andy had already booked our flights and our hotels, but we had no other plans than to check with a concierge in each city for interesting places to visit. One of our most memorable experiences of the trip was a tour recommended by our concierge in Bangkok.

We traveled 80 miles by bus northwest from the city through the countryside of Thailand to the original bridge that was earlier fictionalized in the 1957 Hollywood film, *Bridge on the River Kwai*. During WWII, the bridge was built by the Japanese using forced laborers and Allied prisoners of war as the infamous Burma Railway. Reportedly, nearly half the prisoners working on the project died from disease, maltreatment and accidents. We walked only halfway across the bridge because it was in such poor condition we didn't want to fall into the muddy and swiftly flowing Mae Klong River below.

In Kanchanaburi, we visited two museums commemorating the dead and the Kanchanaburi War Cemetery. We walked among rows and rows of hundreds of neatly placed, white gravestones. Each stone marked the final resting place of a brave American or British soldier. Most of them were in their early 20s to mid-30s. Although Andy and I were born during World War II, and our families had been affected by the war, his family especially, we knew little about how the war had affected the people of Asia. We also hadn't realized how many American soldiers died in this part of Asia. Seeing so many graves of young men whose lives were cut short in defense of our freedom was a sobering and unforgettable experience.

Once we returned to Riyadh, we were relieved to learn Andy's educational leave had been approved. Thus, we hastily made final preparations for our trip back home. I left Riyadh before Andy so I could spend time in Hillsdale with John and Bob, and in Worthington with my mother and sister Marcia and her family. I would fly to San Francisco, my first trip ever to the legendary 'City by The Bay' where Andy and his brother George would meet me. We spent a few days in Vacaville with George, Nancy, Erika and Matt and Andy's parents, who were visiting at the time from Grand Haven. From there, we flew to Seattle for Andy's meeting and afterward to Detroit. We rented a car in Detroit and drove to Ann Arbor to see Peter at the University of Michigan and to Lansing to visit Leis at Michigan State University. From Detroit, we flew to Chicago where my sister Barbara and our brother-in-law Jim met us at the airport for a quick visit before we left for New York. From New York, we flew back to Riyadh—one last time.

While in California visiting Andy's brother and our sister-in-law, they handed us an article from the *San Francisco Chronicle* dated September 30, 1990. Written by Marianne Alireza, the article was titled, *Behind the Veil*. Reading it, I knew why Marianne had made such an impression on me when I met and spoke with her earlier. Respectful of tradition, she was nonetheless a champion for equal rights and opportunities for males and females and for perceiving life as a positive adventure rather than a battle between good and evil. What follows are the opening paragraphs of her full-page article.

> *Taught for centuries that God wanted members of their sex to stay home, Saudi Arabian women have been shocked in recent days to open their newspapers and find pictures of American women soldiers roaming about their country. Shocked—and excited.*
>
> *"Maybe it will start more people here thinking about how we women could help ease our own Saudi labor shortage," says an oil-company employee—and a wife and mother—whom I know in Dhahran. "If nothing else, we could take certain jobs that would release our men for other work."*
>
> *The Saudi government is thinking along the same lines. On September 3, King Fahad, in a directive aimed at freeing more men for military service, ordered government agencies to "accept those women volunteers who present themselves to carry on duties in the areas of human services and medical services within the context of fully preserving Islamic and social values."*
>
> *For a culture that until a few years ago strictly prohibited any public contact between men and women, and still requires women to wear concealing garments in public, the edict was striking: After all, it came from the highest authority in this conservative Muslim society, not from the liberal fringe that has for years pressed for a greater role for women.*
>
> *Saudi women have long been free to serve other women in such roles as nurses, gynecologists or teachers in girls' schools.*
>
> *Now female doctors and nurses may be able to care for male hospital patients or work as clerks in banks and stores with male clienteles. [sic].*

There is even talk about women helping ambulance and fire-fighting units. "Before the crisis with Iraq, this would have been blasphemy," said a Saudi government official.

As soon as we returned to Riyadh, I noticed a further decline in the morale among hospital staff. The changes Marianne and many other educated Saudis and non-Saudis, Muslims and non-Muslims were hoping for were not coming easily. Such radical changes occur over many years, sometimes two, three, four generations—or more. Expats who were staying at King Fahad didn't feel they're being appreciated enough by Administration. In spite of the risks, they weren't receiving an increase in pay. Administration also cut some benefits, such as free dental care. We heard rumors that a new incentive package was coming out soon giving bonuses to physicians (not nurses or techs), plus life insurance policies replacing those now invalid because we were in a war zone.

The best news I heard when we came back from the U.S. was that if there was a war, it wouldn't start until late January. It seemed careless to tell the world when you planned to strike your enemy. What did I know about war? Only that I didn't want to be in the middle of one. We were scheduled to leave on the evening of January 9th since that was the end of Andy's contract. *Dear Lord,* I prayed and prayed, *please keep us safe until then.*

A few days after we returned to Riyadh, Andy noticed a worrisome absence of English newspapers. All newspapers in the MC grocery store and the hospital gift shop were in Arabic. We suspected something had happened or was about to happen that the authorities didn't want Westerners to know, so we tuned into the BBC on our broadband radio. My sister Barbara filled us in on details when she called from Chicago on Friday morning.

Apparently, a group of fifty Saudi females drove through downtown Riyadh on November 6th to protest their country's ban on women driving. For half an hour, they drove their cars in a convoy around the city until stopped by police. The women paid dearly for their actions. All the drivers—and their husbands—were banned for a year from foreign travel. The women who had government jobs were fired. From hundreds of mosques, muezzins were denouncing them by name as immoral females out to destroy Saudi society. A few of the more radical muezzins were calling for their heads.

The next day, Suhair and I were working quietly at our desks when the door to our office flew open, slamming against the wall. In rushed eight, fully covered, veiled females. The last one in shut the door and locked it behind her. They all flipped back their veils and looked for a place to sit. Shocked by this bold and unexpected intrusion, Suhair and I gave up our chairs and moved to one corner of the room. Several of the women sat on our desks; a few sat on the floor. Suhair whispered translations to me since I couldn't understand what the women were saying.

"It's about the driving," Suhair said softly. "Some say driving was good; others say timing was bad. Saudi Arabia's conservative religious forces are furious about non-Muslim American troops being here. By driving, they've pushed back any reform of women's rights in Saudi Arabia at least fifty years. These women are angry because they're powerless to do anything. They feel betrayed by their own kind because a small group of women acted on their behalf. It not only failed; it backfired to affect all females. They say women have no way of uniting because it's against the law for women to meet in groups."

"Who are these women? I don't recognize any of them. Where did they come from?" I whispered.

"I'm not sure why they're here at the hospital," Suhair said. "It's unusual and dangerous. I hope they leave soon because if someone from Administration finds them here, you and I could be in trouble."

Five minutes later, the women pulled down their veils and left as quickly and as mysteriously as they appeared. We heard later via the grapevine that several female drivers were college-educated Saudis, many well-traveled and married to successful, well-respected Saudis. While some said their husbands supported their demonstration, other husbands divorced their wives immediately for bringing shame to their families. The women drove because they feared a war would deplete the number of male drivers available, and they didn't want to stand helplessly by at a time of crisis for their country.

The next day, Mr. Al Senaidy, now back from his lengthy leave-of-absence, called me into his office. It wasn't the first time I had seen him since his return, so I assumed this wasn't a friendly 'long-time-no-see' kind of meeting.

"Pam, what do you think about the females driving?" he said in a rather gruff voice.

Remembering my mother's admonition to 'keep my eyes and ears open and my mouth shut', I simply said, "I don't have an opinion, Mr. Al Senaidy. I've been too busy planning for the next issue of *The Bulletin* to be worried about something I know nothing about."

I understood that Mr. Al Senaidy wanted to make sure I wasn't expressing views that might appear disrespectful, or create problems between his staff in Public Affairs and Administration at such a sensitive time.

Another American expat, a computer programmer, expressed views of the driving fiasco this way: "First tell me I'll be safe from the war and that no one will get killed and that the crisis has been settled; then we'll talk about women driving in Saudi Arabia."

Once again, T.E. Lawrence's well known quote came to mind: *Better for them to do it imperfectly than for me to do it perfectly; it is their country, their war and my time here is limited.*

Repeating these words to myself helped me maintain equanimity during the driving event that led to other problems, such as the one described in the following notice we received from our American neighbor.

On November 15th, some forty mutawa raided a party in a private villa in Riyadh. Armed with guns, clubs and axes, mutawa climbed over the villa walls, knocking down men and women. One mutawa allegedly held a 38-caliber pistol to the head of an American citizen when he tried to aid a woman on the ground being kicked by another mutawa. This same American allegedly attempted to leave the villa approximately forty-five minutes earlier, but three mutawa ordered him back into the villa. Another mutawa pulled an American woman out from under a table by her hair, slapped her, and tried to rip off her blouse. Later, after the arrival of the police, mutawa rounded up guests at the party. Twenty-two men, including two American citizens, were placed in a small room without electricity or water. Periodically, during the night, buckets of water were thrown through the window onto the men inside. At 7:00 the next morning, the men were transferred to Malaz Police Station. The twenty-six women, including the above-mentioned American citizen, were taken to a separate room for interrogation before transfer to the Women's Prison. The American Embassy strongly protests the unnecessary force and violent brutality exhibited by the mutawa toward American citizens and requests Ministry to take steps to assure that there will be no repetition of such activities in the future.

I shuddered to think Andy and I could have experienced the same outcome had any mutawa raided a party we attended. Our host was a Saudi prince who invited his friends and their guests for an evening of Western-style music, dancing and socializing with expats and Saudis. Located in a middle-class neighborhood on the outskirts of Riyadh, the entrance to the bunker-type, party house was unlit and unmarked. Sealed from the outside by thick, soundproof double doors, the bar, dance floor and party room were underground and lit with soft twinkling lights as music played in the background.

Reminiscent of a scene from a dance club back home, men and women in smart casual dress stood conversing with each other and enjoying drinks and hors d'oeuvres. Some were dancing to popular songs such as *Miss You Much* by Janet Jackson, *We Didn't Start the Fire* by Billy Joel, and *Another Day in Paradise* by Phil Collins. The irony of the song titles didn't escape me, considering what was going on in Riyadh at the time.

The fully stocked bar offered whatever a guest might want: hard liquor, wine, beer, soft drinks. Andy had several glasses of wine, and I had a glass of champagne. No one I saw was 'over-served' or exhibiting poor behavior. We met some fascinating couples and individuals, including the prince, who couldn't have been more gracious and welcoming.

Andy and I danced together a few times not knowing if we'd ever have an opportunity to dance in the desert again. When we left, the contrast between the lively party inside and the quiet neighborhood outside was remarkable. Once the soundproof, double-width outside door closed behind us, no sounds escaped the party scene. As we made our way in absolute silence in the dark to our car, we realized how foolish we had been. Fortunately, we made it back to our compound without being stopped by police or mutawa. We promised each other we would never again drink alcohol in Saudi Arabia, regardless of who tempted us to indulge.

Prior to our evening at the prince's party, our view of such incidents was a bit self-righteous. We thought anyone ignoring the cultural differences in this strict Muslim culture shouldn't complain if caught by religious police. Men and women of any culture or citizenship who socialized together while enjoying homemade or black-market alcoholic beverages had to know they were exposing themselves to serious repercussions. While it never occurred to me when Andy and I came to Riyadh not to abide by their rules, we learned how easy it was to break them.

A few weeks later, at the American Embassy, I met an articulate, well-educated, young Saudi woman, the wife of a Saudi diplomat. She first came to the U.S. as a college student at age nineteen, with little knowledge of American culture in the 1980s.

"My mental image of American males was they were all cowboys," she said.

What follows are her exact words that day when we met over a cup of tea. I took notes as she described her life as a naive and inexperienced Saudi female in America, away from her family and culture for the first time. She admitted to feelings of isolation and fear because the less restricted cultural mores for females in America were so different from those in Saudi Arabia.

"In the Middle East, girls hung out with girls only. I had no experience socializing with boys. My education began when my parents left me in Washington D.C. in a co-ed dorm (she didn't say what college). I was timid and didn't know how to handle myself. My first pajama party, I wore silk PJ's and people made fun of me. Everyone was drinking alcohol, which is against my religion as a Muslim; women were wearing the smallest PJ's or not wearing anything. To me, this was degrading and embarrassing. I couldn't behave like them. I felt so out of place, and I didn't know what to do. I was afraid to tell my parents. Boyfriends stayed all night with girls. Items disappeared from my room. I couldn't leave money in my room. I had no car. I couldn't drive anyway. In Saudi Arabia, my mother always told me what to do. In Beirut, same. In the U.S., I was treated like an adult. The first six months were horrible. I refused dates. It was considered taboo to go out on dates in my culture. No drinking, no drugs. I was not welcome in the dorm. It was a stressful time for me. Men thought I was snobbish or queer.

"I finally moved to an international female dorm. My roommate was Arab—Jordanian— and she understood and respected my ways. I hated America then, but I wanted to graduate. I didn't tell everyone back home what I was going through because they would be scared for me. I wasn't in any danger; I was just unhappy. My other roommate, who was Chinese, wanted me to integrate into U.S. society. All I wanted was for her to accept me as I was—as I am. I was so attached to my country and culture. In another building, people accepted me as an international student. I didn't take offense at their curiosity. Gradually, I came to learn that we are different. I didn't translate [sic] from my perceptions. I accepted people as they were. My culture shock was so severe I didn't want to socialize with Americans. I didn't want to lose my identity, but I wanted to know them through firsthand experience. Books only tell what the writer believes. We are all different, as all Americans are different.

"My advice to anyone traveling to another country and culture is to meet people yourself. Don't listen to someone else's opinions and evaluations. Make up your own mind based on your own experiences and values. Be objective. Accept other cultures as they are. Appreciate differences. Ask Americans about their culture; don't ask Saudis who are visiting the U.S. about American culture. Accept the fact that you're in a different culture and be proud of who you are. Different is different, not wrong or bad. Enjoy the differences; learn from them to have a broader, richer knowledge and understanding of the human family.

"Women's rights in Saudi Arabia is a hot issue now. We have odd feelings. I have them, too. Culture shock can be confusing to you. We're all people after all. We have the same feelings, the same basic human needs."

"Do you believe women in Saudi Arabia will be given the right to drive?" I asked.

"No. I don't believe there will be major change anytime soon. I don't see women driving here for a long, long time."

The following week, I attended yet another morning coffee at the American Embassy. Our speaker was a female pilot with the Air National Guard, born in California, stationed at Sawyer Air Force Base in Northern Michigan. She flew a modified DC-10 refueling aircraft and had 1,500 hours of flight time. She was single, small in stature and attractive. Her saving grace was her sense of humor; she couldn't have done her job without one.

"I didn't get many briefings about being female in Saudi Arabia," she told the audience of American women. "What a surprise to learn the male Saudi air traffic controller at the airport wouldn't talk to me because I was female. My co-pilot has to do all the talking over the radio. I only have to fly the plane and make sure takeoff, refueling, and landing go well."

With Thanksgiving just a few days away, we were delighted to be invited to Don and Millie-Lynn's for Thanksgiving dinner. Just back from a holiday in Africa, Millie-Lynn's decision to host a Thanksgiving Dinner for eight was last minute. Still, she spoiled us all with her gourmet culinary skills and quintessential hospitality. It was a diverse group: Elsie and Michael (Lebanese), Freda and Milt (Greek), Don and Millie-Lynn (Canadian) and

Andy and I (American). With such an interesting group, the conversation was lively and thought provoking. As most expatriates at intimate gatherings who trust each other, we covered topics from females driving to the King's interesting relationship with mutawa.

Michael, the Lebanese businessman, said the King pays 15,000 active mutawa in Riyadh for hassling errant Muslims and unlawful non-Muslims. The subject of last week's raid came up. Although he didn't reveal his source, he said French, American, Canadian and other Western professionals in their thirties, both married couples, and singles, were having a masalama[20] party. Homemade alcoholic drinks such as beer and wine were available. Forty mutawa spotted the catering van and followed it to the villa, climbed over the walls surrounding the villa and beat down the front door. Married couples were allowed to leave after showing proof of marriage. Single people were rounded up and taken to jail. An American friend of a friend said she spent twenty-four hours in jail and was well treated compared to other women who were beaten and had their clothes torn off. Reportedly, one woman was beaten with the heel of her high-heeled shoe. The room they stayed in had bunks but no sheets or blankets. A hole in the middle of the floor served as the toilet.

The invasion plus Thanksgiving and Christmas, with U.S. military personnel shopping in the malls, put mutawa on high alert. Such distractions were taking their toll on people's lives. The American Embassy canceled all social activities. Christmas celebrations would be extra low-key this year. When Andy and I told everyone we were leaving at the end of Andy's contract in January, Millie-Lynn understood but Elsie tried to talk us into

---

[20] Goodbye

staying. Minutes earlier, Elsie had shared one of her stories about life in the Kingdom after living 20 years as an expat in Riyadh.

"If a female is injured in an automobile accident, no male is allowed to touch her to give her emergency treatment. It's also illegal for a male to load her into an ambulance if she needs to go to the hospital," said Elsie.

Elsie had told me this before, one of the reasons I turned down Freda's offer to work at the princesses' school. I truly loved Elsie and valued her friendship, but I wondered why she thought being reminded of this might persuade me to change my mind about leaving.

Chapter 19

Masalama

In the months, weeks and days before my first trip to Saudi Arabia, I lived by the calendar. I kept it next to my place on the breakfast table at 901 Spruce Street in Petoskey, counting the days until Andy came home. Every night before I went to bed, I relished crossing off another day with a black magic marker. Now, as we began our countdown to January 9th, I found myself living by the calendar again. The days were filling up fast with masalama parties and tasks I needed to accomplish before departure. I kept the calendar on our breakfast table along with my to-do list and consulted both every morning. At dinnertime, I delighted in crossing off tasks completed and another day gone by, which made me feel closer to home.

Our other constant companion at the breakfast table was our broadband radio. First one down the stairs each morning would tune into the BBC for updates on the situation in the Gulf. One day, the news would give us hope that peace might prevail; next day, peace seemed unlikely. Good news came the end of November when the United Nations Security Council passed a resolution authorizing member states "to use all necessary means to uphold and implement all previous resolutions demanding the immediate withdrawal of Iraq from Kuwait." The goal of the resolution was to give Saddam Hussein one last, firm message that the United Nations would not allow Iraq to continue its occupation of Kuwait. Even its close ally and former enemy of the U.S., the Soviet Union, tried to convince Saddam to reconsider his actions. Soviet premier Mikhail Gorbachev tried to persuade Saddam to look out for his own and Iraq's best interests. He was successful in having fellow U.N. member states include a period of goodwill within the resolution. This was designed to give Iraq an opportunity to review its policy and actions, and hopefully come to the conclusion that it would be best to withdraw and avoid this escalating crisis.

Andy thought Saddam would withdraw his troops from Kuwait and regroup his forces to make big trouble later on for the entire Middle East. Based on prognostications from folks throughout the hospital and beyond, Andy believed the days were numbered for the House of Saud. After hearing from several reputable sources that the royal family was in the process of transferring massive amounts of wealth to foreign banks, Andy said it seemed likely King Fahad and other senior royals would flee. How people gleaned insider information, I had no idea; nor did I care, except if by knowing it, and it was accurate, we were able to get out of there before war.

Once again, our Christmas would be subdued this year. We would have no tree, no gifts and no decorations. Instead, we were busy baking, scheduling parties, and writing Christmas and 'holiday' cards, depending on whether the recipient was Christian, Muslim or Jewish. It felt strange to prepare for Christmas while preparing for war. Everything that couldn't fit into our two suitcases was already on its way to Andy's parents' home in Grand Haven. Janet, Peggye and I baked cookies for the American Women in Riyadh coffee for American service men and women. Andy and I were planning to co-host a homemade, traditional Christmas dinner at Janet and Dick's villa for ten U.S. soldiers, along with three other American couples.

Andy and I were delighted to receive invitations to two masalama parties given in our honor by unlikely hosts. The first invitation came from Andy's Saudi resident in rheumatology and internal medicine.

"Finally, we get to experience a relaxed, informal dinner with a Saudi couple, just the four of us, in their home," I said with delight. "Plus, Mohammed is bi-lingual so even if his wife doesn't speak English, we can still communicate. No segregation of sexes. I can't wait. How wonderful that this is happening before we leave."

Andy said the couple was young and had a one-year-old son. As we drove across the desert to the other side of Riyadh where the family lived, I could hardly contain my excitement. When we arrived at their home, the exterior looked similar to our villa, surrounded by a high wall made of tan, stucco-like material. The gate was open, so we drove into the large courtyard and walked together to the front entrance. Andy knocked on the door as his colleague opened it and greeted Andy by extending his hand.

"Mohammed, this is my wife, Pam," Andy said.

Mohammed bowed but did not extend his hand. I had a feeling our evening would not be 'Westernized' after all. Mohammed opened a nearby door and motioned for me to enter, pulling the door shut behind him. A young female, presumably his wife, came walking toward me from across the dimly lit room, smiling and extending her hand.

"Masaa al-khair," she said.

"Masaa al-noor," I answered.

"Kayf haalik?"

"Tayib-wa. Shukran[21]."

In spite of having had Arabic lessons at the hospital, speaking Arabic still felt awkward to me. I could greet people, say please and thank you, count to twenty, and ask directions to a female toilet. I knew a few words and phrases but couldn't carry on an extended conversation. I sadly realized her

---

[21] Good evening; Good evening; How are you? Fine, thank you.

English was about as good as my Arabic.

The young hostess motioned for me to sit on a pillow next to a low table in the middle of the room. A TV stood against one wall with the volume turned up and a full-screen shot of a Saudi male speaking Arabic. A single light bulb hanging from the ceiling was the only illumination, other than the television. For the next two hours, the wife who did not speak English proudly brought out a variety of dishes for me to try, mostly pureed vegetables. I ate alone, trying to ignore the noise from the TV, since the wife never stayed to eat with me. My only social diversion was their little son who was learning to walk and talk. Smiling at me and jabbering, he would cruise in and out of the kitchen on his tippy toes, rolling across the hardwood floor in his walker on wheels. I waved and smiled back at him. An older woman I assumed to be the mother or mother-in-law appeared periodically at the kitchen door, smiling at me. All I could do was smile back and bring my hands together in front of my chest, bowing my head in a gesture of gratitude. Sitting on the floor and eating alone while watching a TV program I didn't understand was a far different experience than I had anticipated. I assumed we would have an enlightening and open conversation between Andy and me and a Saudi couple so I could better understand their culture. Instead, I couldn't wait for the evening to end.

Finally, Mohammed stuck only his head in the room.

"Mrs. Daugavietis?"

"Yes," I answered and quickly rose to my feet, stretching out my legs one at a time to make sure I could walk after sitting so long. I crossed the room to shake hands with the hostess, now standing in the kitchen doorway. In my smile and handshake, I hoped she could feel my appreciation of her hospitality without betraying the bewilderment I felt over the fact that we never engaged in conversation. I smiled and waved to the older woman who stood in the background, and patted the little boy on the head. Mohammed walked Andy and me to the front door where we thanked him for his and the family's hospitality and bid him good evening. On the way home, I talked nonstop about my strange situation with the young wife, the mother or mother-in-law, and the baby boy.

"I had better rapport with the little boy than with the females," I said. "At least he and I could play patty-cake and peek-a-boo."

"Wasn't the lamb delicious?" Andy asked.

"Lamb. What lamb? All I had was cooked vegetables."

"Yes, lamb. Best I ever tasted."

A week later, gender roles were reversed at a party given in my honor. Nora, the Saudi female who worked as a translator for Public Affairs hosted a females-only gathering at her apartment in downtown Riyadh. Andy drove me to Nora's high-rise, rode up on the elevator with me to the fifteenth floor and walked me to Nora's front door. He waited until the door opened enough for Suhair to see it was me without Andy seeing her. Andy said he'd be back in two hours and left. As soon as he was out of sight, Suhair opened the door and greeted me with the typical two-cheek, air-kiss greeting and welcomed me into the foyer.

At the hospital, Suhair maintained a subdued demeanor, wearing little makeup and always the hijab. Tonight, she looked much younger with her gorgeous black hair curled around her shoulders and the right amount of makeup to accentuate her dark eyes. She wore gold earrings and a gold, bejeweled necklace with her full-length, violet-colored gown embroidered in gold. When I complimented her, she beamed with appreciation.

When she and I walked into the living room, I was delighted to see Nora, Hala and Nabiha, as well as several unfamiliar faces. Nora introduced me to her sister and two female cousins. Like Suhair, all were wearing jewelry, makeup and modest but stylish and colorful clothing. We visited for a while and then Nora turned on her stereo with drum and flute music similar to the tribal music at Ahmed's wedding. One of Nora's young cousins began dancing, moving her hips like the young females at the wedding, only she brandished a long, elegantly engraved silver sword. Nora said the sword belonged to her grandfather who rode with King Abdul Aziz when he made his legendary raid on horseback to regain control of his family's ancestral fort in Riyadh. The cousin came toward me and took my hand as an invitation to dance with her. All the other women were clapping and laughing, I hoped not at us but with us, as the drumming continued.

    Nora announced it was time to eat so we all made our way to the dining room. There, an abundance of traditional Arabic cuisine awaited us, including roast lamb and chicken, an assortment of vegetables, salads, Arabic bread and hummus, and several trays of sweets. We helped ourselves and took our plates back to the living room where we ate and enjoyed more conversation. As people finished their meal, Nora caught my attention from the far corner of the room and motioned for me to join her. I put down my plate and walked into the kitchen. She reached into an overhead cupboard and pulled out a small glass bottle filled with a clear liquid.

    "Here, Pam, this is for you."

    "What is it, Nora?"

    "You know," she said, smiling. "Try some." She removed the cap and handed it to me.

    "I don't know what it is."

    "Taste it, you'll see. You'll like it, I'm sure."

    Not wanting to seem impolite, I took a small sip. I started coughing and couldn't stop. It was the strongest liquor I had ever tasted.

    "Sorry. I thought you'd like it," Nora said with obvious

disappointment. "I thought all American women drank alcohol."

"Oh, Nora," I said, touched by her misguided yet sincere gesture of hospitality. "Not all American women drink or even like alcohol. You were thoughtful to get this for me because I know it's a risk for you to have it in your home. I don't drink hard liquor. I'm sorry."

Nora said she understood and put the bottle back in her cupboard. I returned to the living room and sat on the couch next to Suhair as Nora went into the dining room. A few minutes later, Nora brought out a beautifully wrapped box and handed it to me.

"It's from all of us; we bought it at the hospital gift shop," she said.

I opened the box to find a crystal and gold camel inside, complete with a rider on top holding a camel whip.

"Oh, I love it, everyone," I said. "Thank you so much. When I'm back home in Michigan, this elegant camel will be a treasured reminder of a memorable evening. "

I deeply appreciated the unexpected kindness shown by this small group of women who had become my friends and confidants at the hospital. All of them were Muslim, yet I felt a kinship with each one. I knew I would miss them and always remember the special friendship we shared, regardless of our differing religious beliefs and cultural traditions.

Several days later, I had lunch at the Medical City restaurant with several other American and Canadian expat wives. The topic of conversation, as usual, focused on the possibility of war and when and if to get out. Many expressed a desire to leave but not without their husbands. Half of them had young children living with them on the compound. I could relate to those feelings and, for the first time, was grateful our kids weren't with us. When I mentioned that Andy's contract ended January 10th, the day we planned to leave, Jean spoke up.

"A reliable source told me the airport is closing January 10th. If you're not out by then, you won't get out."

"I heard the deadline for dependents getting out is January 15th, not the 10th," said another Pam.

So many rumors swirled around the hospital—too many to take any of them seriously. Our only credible source was the American Embassy, and they weren't saying anything except that the threat to Americans was relatively low. Their latest bulletin stated there was no specific, credible information regarding planned terrorist activity in Saudi Arabia. We were advised to be alert to our surroundings, check our house and car for unfamiliar packages, and curtail unnecessary trips outside homes or offices. All we could do was wait and see.

On December 18th, the British government released a travel advisory and ordered all non-essential dependents to return to their homes in the U.K. Within a day or two, the Irish and Swedish embassies followed suit. The Canadians and Americans were waiting to hear what their governments intended to do, which added to everyone's anxiety. The new managing company said they would pay for plane fares home for citizens whose governments had issued travel advisories.

Christmas Eve morning, Nora came to work and said mutawa had called for the elimination of limousine drivers for females. No more females, single or married, riding in a limousine without a male family member chaperone. Otherwise, the day was quiet and uneventful. While this latest edict wouldn't affect me, I knew it would have major repercussions on expat females who stayed, as well as local females.

That evening, Andy and I celebrated alone, in our villa, as we had last year. We read the Christmas story from the Bible, lit our Mary candle for a few minutes, and listened to our Boney M tape. The next morning, I was delighted to find a handful of Christmas cards in our mailbox at the hospital, most of them from home. One was from Tav, from the Philippines, signed by him and his wife, Rita.

That weekend, we were invited to three Christmas parties on the compound. Many of our good friends had already gone, so we were grateful a few friends remained. Andy was on call New Year's Eve, so we spent a quiet evening at home. We also attended several New Year's parties the following weekend, but people's moods at all the gatherings were subdued. Expat wives, especially, were frustrated by the uncertainties, about not being able to make plans. Everything was in flux and changing day-by-day, almost hour-by-hour. The mood at the hospital had deteriorated to cautiously pessimistic. People smiled as they passed each other in the halls but not in the carefree way they greeted each other when we first arrived.

Elsie and Michael called and insisted on bringing us a home-cooked, Lebanese masalama dinner. Elsie knew we were trying to clean out our cupboards and refrigerator and that our kitchen was bare. Three days before our departure, at dinnertime, they arrived at our front door with two large baskets of food. They brought Elsie's hummus, kebabs, fried eggplant, homemade pickles, Arabic bread and a layered gelatin salad, a specialty of Elsie's, along with a box of bakery sweets. When we said goodbye that evening, Elsie and I hugged tightly.

"We'll always keep you in the sweetest corner of our memories," she said.

Once again, I was touched by the intensity of the friendships we formed in a relatively brief span of time. We had met Elsie and Michael at Freda and Milt's dinner party soon after we arrived. We celebrated with them when their daughter Sharmine married a Lebanese physician practicing in Bahrain, and when she later became pregnant with their first grandchild. I knew in my heart of hearts I would never see Elsie again; yet, I would never forget her or the bond we shared. Perhaps it was the threat of impending war that made my farewell with Elsie and other good friends so sad. When I came to Saudi Arabia, I never dreamed I would have friends who meant so much to me. Now, leaving them behind was a loss I hadn't anticipated.

The next morning, the Brits issued gas masks to all their citizens. I had made arrangements to meet my friend, Rosemary, a dietician, in the cafeteria for a good-bye lunch. Her gas mask was securely clipped to the belt of her white uniform. Rosemary told me her son called from the U.K. that morning to tell her to come home. Rosemary came to Riyadh as a single woman and fell in love with a Saudi named Mohammed.

"I told my son I wouldn't leave without Mohammed, and Mohammed won't leave," she said.

I thought of Bob calling earlier telling me to come home, and how I didn't want to leave without Andy. I could relate to Rosemary's feelings and was glad I wasn't in her shoes.

"I brought you a little gift," Rosemary said as she handed me an unwrapped book, *The Road From Coorain* by Jill Ker Conway. "I loved reading it and hope you will, too. It's about a woman like us who left home looking for love and adventure."

We hugged and said goodbye. I told her I'd send her a note to let her know what I thought of the book. Little did I know that I would read every page on the way home to New York, and how much the book would continue to inspire me some twenty-five years later.

On Monday, my good American friend Diane Fugello surprised me by calling at work.

"Only ten more to go."

"What do you mean?"

"Ten more prayer calls before you leave. Aren't you excited?"

"Oh, you bet I am. I can't wait."

It would be another bittersweet parting because Diane and Fuge and their boys were staying. Diane knew how eager I was to leave, and she was happy for us. She never expressed any fear for herself and her family, only joy for us to be returning to our families and a new life together. She was that kind of a friend who could be happy for someone else, even when times were tough for her. I had a feeling they weren't leaving because if they did Fuge would be out of a job and if Fuge couldn't leave, they weren't leaving either. You learn a lot about a person when you see their attitude and how they choose to behave in a crisis. Some time later, a mutual expat friend told me Diane died of cancer shortly after the family returned home, after the Gulf War. This heartbreaking news was yet another reminder to live each day in gratitude. I will always be grateful for the memories I have of Diane and our special friendship in Saudi Arabia.

My last day of work was Tuesday, January 8th. That morning, Andy and I listened to a BBC report about the Geneva Peace Conference taking place the next day in Switzerland between U.S. Secretary of State James Baker and Iraq's Foreign Minister Tariq Aziz. The hope was that they could reach a peaceful agreement to avoid a war between Iraq and the U.S.-backed coalition of 34 other nations, with the U.S. taking the lead. Not much hope was resting on this meeting, the final peace initiative. On my way to my office in Ward 16, I bumped into my friend Aisha, a nurse in ENT.

"Good-bye, Aisha," I said. "Andy and I are leaving tomorrow. I'll miss you. I wish you and your family well."

"Oh, Pam, please don't leave tomorrow especially. It's not safe to travel tomorrow. The talks in Switzerland are taking place and they might trigger some reaction that would make it dangerous for you to fly."

I assured Aisha we would be fine, but I knew I couldn't be certain about anything anymore, except the power of prayer.

When I walked into Public Affairs, Mr. Al Senaidy greeted me with a welcoming smile.

"It's not too late to cancel your plans to leave," he said, as he twirled his prayer beads. "We'd love to have you stay. You know how much work we have here. You like to be busy. You'll be sorry if you leave."

Suhair, standing next to Mr. Al Senaidy, spoke up. "Saddam doesn't know it yet, but the West is serious. When he does, he'll leave Kuwait. We want you to stay."

"When Saddam backs down, everyone can forget their plans to leave," Mr. Al Senaidy added.

I thanked them for their kind encouragement but assured them our plans to leave were firm. I spent the rest of my last day cleaning out my desk, going for coffee several times to the cafeteria, and visiting people throughout the hospital to say goodbye one last time.

I was deeply touched to find two 'Season's Greetings' cards in our hospital mailbox. One was signed, "Good-bye and Good Luck, Love, Nabiha." The other was signed, "Much love, Helen."

Of all my friends at the hospital, Suhair was the one I cared about the most. Suhair's life was easier than many Egyptian women but difficult by U.S. standards. Later that afternoon, she was waiting for me in our office with a beautifully wrapped gift. I was so self-absorbed in panic mode that I hadn't thought about buying her a gift as a lasting token of our friendship. Suhair gave me two small, metal vases, etched with an attractive, Egyptian-looking black, copper and silver design. I loved them immediately and knew they would always have a special place in our new home.

Chapter 20

Going Home

On our day of departure, I awoke with mixed emotions. I felt joyful excitement, nervous anxiety, and, yes, sadness, too. As obsessively as I had counted the days before we could leave, I was surprised by my sentimental mood. I walked through all the empty rooms in our villa, pausing to recall memories from our first day here. I was a new bride then, a new stepmother, a middle-aged woman in search of herself, who also found in the Arabian Desert happiness, adventure, friendships, and the beginnings of a career as a writer. I gazed out the windows at our neighborhood, knowing I would never come back to this place again. I wanted always to remember this special time Andy and I shared together as husband and wife, but I couldn't wait to get home to our children, our families, and to our real lives in America.

A few remaining friends on the compound, Peggye, Janet, Diane, Millie-Lynn and Theresa had planned an informal goodbye luncheon at MC. Everyone's mood was positive; we purposely avoided war talk. Instead, we mostly laughed, recounting some of our fondest memories and craziest experiences. They surprised me with a pair of gold earrings. We promised to all stay in touch.

Our plane was scheduled to leave Riyadh at 9:45 p.m. Administration advised us to leave our keys on the kitchen counter and lock our villa when we left for the airport. It was 6:45 p.m. when the limousine pulled in front of our villa, and we closed the door for the last time. At that moment, we were homeless and without passports. A fellow named Abdullah in staff services told us Mohammed would meet us at the airport with our passports, standard operating procedure for departing expats. We were naive to believe him.

Chaos greeted us at the airport. I had never seen such a diverse mass of humanity in one place or heard such clamor—people yelling, babies crying, announcements blaring over the loud speaker in Arabic. Before us were the fleeing citizenry of Riyadh—countless men, non-Saudi Middle Easterners for the most part, wearing turbans and carrying boxes and soft bundles tied together with rope, veiled females carrying babies, small children carrying blankets and holding hands, all with terrified looks on their faces, many in tears.

We scanned the crowd for Mohammed. Abdullah said he would be waiting for us near the Saudia ticket counter. Andy stood five feet away from where I waited with our bags, looking for the man who held our very lives in his hands. Without our passports, we couldn't check in. If we didn't check in soon, we wouldn't leave. I watched the minute hands on the clock overhead move from 8:00 to 8:15 to 8:30. Still no sign of Mohammed.

"Andy, call Administration. Call someone. Find Mohammed," I shouted loudly enough for Andy to hear me above all the commotion. "If we don't get those passports, we're not getting out of here."

Andy hurried to a nearby pay phone. I continued to watch for Mohammed as Andy called the hospital. When I glanced over to see if he was able to reach anyone, his grim expression crushed my hopes. All I could do was close my eyes and pray.

Dear God, thank you for bringing us this far. We must leave tonight, or we won't get out before the war. Many others also want to be on that plane when it leaves. Please get all of us out safely.

"The guy I spoke with said Mohammed should have been here half an hour ago," Andy said when he came back.

We stood by our luggage in silence, helpless to do anything but wait. I was too angry to cry. Fifteen anxious minutes later, here comes Mohammed, sauntering aimlessly through the crowd, grinning from ear to ear. Without apology, explanation or sense of urgency, he handed over our passports. I have never been so happy to hold such a small, yet so essential, object in my hands. Relieved beyond words, I simply smiled at Mohammed. Andy thanked him in Arabic and shook his hand. We gathered our bags and hurried to the end of the line in front of the Saudia check-in counter.

"You'll have to hurry. The plane is full," the agent said. "No seat assignments."

We grabbed our carry-ons and ran as fast as we could without bumping into other passengers making their way to the departure gate. Once up the stairs and through the front entrance of the 747, it was a free-for-all. People were elbowing each other to get seats together. We spotted two empty seats by a window in the rear of the economy section and made a dash to claim them. Within minutes, all seats in our cabin were taken. In the row across the aisle from us sat two U.S. soldiers, young fellows going on leave.

"Thank you for your service," Andy said as he reached over to shake hands with both of them.

I was so emotional I couldn't speak. I waved and smiled instead. I thought of John and Bob and how glad I was they weren't wearing military uniforms and preparing to fight in any wars. In the row in front of the soldiers sat four Saudi females, all veiled, all holding infants and toddlers crying loudly and inconsolably.

"This may be a long ride," I said to Andy.

Once airborne, we expected to touch down in Jeddah, as before, and then on to New York. We knew the plane was full, but perhaps some of the passengers would get out in Jeddah and others would board. Not so. The pilot announced we were carrying an unusually heavy load—more passengers and cargo than ever before. Thus, we would have only a brief layover in London to refuel, but we were not to leave the plane. He also told us King Khalid Airport closed after we left. Jean was right. The U.S. finally declared a travel advisory.

Andy settled back in his seat to sleep. I couldn't stop thinking about the chaos we had just escaped, and how grateful I was that we were leaving. I prayed for those left behind, for a safe flight ahead, and for war in the Middle East to be avoided. I thought about seeing John and Bob again, my mother and everyone else who had written so faithfully while we were away. It broke my heart to have to burn every piece of mail we had received before we left. We couldn't fit it in our suitcases or carry-ons. I kept a few letters from the boys and watched the rest of the dozens of cards and letters go up in flames and smoke in the stone-covered courtyard behind our villa.

With a long flight ahead of us, I pulled out the book Rosemary gave me, turned on my overhead light, and settled back in my seat. I had no prior knowledge of Jill Ker Conway, and quickly learned she left her home in Australia to later become the first female president of Smith College. After finishing the first chapter, I couldn't put the book down. Throughout the flight, I continued to read between meals, dozing off occasionally for an hour or so at a time.

Reading Jill Ker Conway's memoir caused me to reflect on my own journey from Worthington, Ohio, to Petoskey, Michigan, to Grand Rapids, Michigan, back to Petoskey, and then to Saudi Arabia and now back to Michigan. A decade ago, I thought my life was over. Now, I truly believed my life was just beginning. I thought about the woman who had become like a second mother to me when I lived in Petoskey. Lillian and Ron Nordstrom were members of First Presbyterian Church and treated me like a daughter. Lillian was always consoling me with her wisdom and compassion when I'd complain about being single and wishing I was in a loving and permanent relationship with a man who truly loved me.

"In God's time, my dear," she would say in her kind and caring way. "Not your time, but God's time."

Ron had passed away, but Lillian was now living in a nursing home in the Detroit area. At our first opportunity, I wanted to visit her and tell her she was right all along. Dreams do come true when you do your best and trust God to take care of the rest, another one of her familiar sayings.

As our plane approached J.F.K., I was so emotional I began to weep. We flew over New York Harbor and saw the Statue of Liberty, the twin towers of the World Trade Center and the Empire State Building. Along with everyone else on board, Andy and I could hardly contain our emotions. Passengers cheered as they strained to look out the windows while staying strapped in their seats. The moment the wheels of our 747 touched down on the runway, passengers erupted in shouts of joy and clapping. I had never felt so patriotic as when we landed in New York that day. I couldn't wait to touch the ground once we disembarked. The babies across the aisle were crying at the top of their lungs. Their mothers were hurriedly gathering up their belongings. We had been on that plane, in our seats, for nearly 18 hours. Once in the international terminal, we only had a few minutes to make one phone call each before claiming our luggage and catching a bus to La Guardia. I called Mother and Andy called his parents. It was 10:00 a.m.

"Mother, we're in New York," I said the minute she picked up the phone. "We're safe. It is so good to hear your voice."

"Pammy, I'm so relieved. How soon do you leave for Grand

Rapids?"

"Our plane leaves La Guardia around 1:00. We make a quick stop in Detroit and should be in Grand Rapids by 4:00 this afternoon. I'll call you as soon as we get to Grand Haven."

The soldiers who sat behind us were waiting for their bags when we got to baggage claim. We overheard them complaining about the babies wailing all the way from Riyadh. Perhaps past experience with our own babies made it easier for us to tune out their familiar cries.

"I'm never getting married," said one soldier. "I'm never having kids," said another. I have often thought of those young fellows, wondering if they ever changed their minds.

The remainder of our long journey home was uneventful. Andy's parents and sister Anita met us at the airport in Grand Rapids. We had been traveling for nearly 27 hours—from the time we left our villa to the time we walked in the front door of Andy's parents' home in Grand Haven. I called Mother first, and then the boys in Hillsdale.

That night in bed, as Andy slept next to me, I couldn't stop thinking about those we left behind, friends and colleagues at the hospital, neighbors on Al Awzae, friends in the writer's group. I thanked God we made it home safely, grateful we had talked with all our kids that day, our parents and siblings. I tried to think of happier, more peaceful times to come—like seeing our kids and family on a more regular basis. We had missed them all and wanted to reconnect with everyone as soon as possible. So many changes had taken place in the interim, in all our lives.

If only we can avoid war, inshallah, inshallah, inshallah, I kept repeating over and over to myself until I eventually surrendered into a deep, and blessed, sleep.

Epilogue

One week to the day after we landed in Grand Rapids, a massive U.S.-led air offensive targeted Iraq. American and other coalition air power hit Iraq's air defenses, moving swiftly to destroy its communications networks, weapons plants, and more. We watched television non-stop as the Iraqis launched Scud missiles into Saudi Arabia and Israel, and U.S. and coalition planes bombed other areas of Iraq. After a while, the horrifying scenes and sounds of innocent citizens being killed and property being destroyed was so upsetting that I quit watching. All I could think about were friends still there as well as thousands of others who couldn't leave for whatever reason. For the first time in my life, I experienced survivor's guilt. Grateful to be home, I grieved for those whose lives and homes were being destroyed, as we watched from the safety and comfort of our own.

A cease-fire was declared February 28, 1991, with an estimated death toll of 10,300, mostly Kuwaitis and Iraqis. The cease-fire did not end the war. While we stayed intensely interested in the aftermath of the war, we had to close that chapter of our lives and shift our focus to the present and future.

All our mementoes—my journals, our 1989-1990 calendars, *Saudi Gazette* newspapers, issues of *The Bulletin*, holiday cards, photographs and books—sat untouched in plastic bins in our basement for years. I had no time to go through them then; we had to get on with our lives. My dear mother had saved my letters to her during our stay in Saudi Arabia, as well as copies of her letters to me, so all of them went into storage, untouched for the next fifteen years.

After September 11, 2001, twelve years to the day after Andy and I became engaged, life became different for many of us. In 1988, it was one of the happiest days of my life. In 2001, it was one of the most terrifying. My thoughts, feelings and memories of that day in 2001 could fill volumes, but are beyond the scope of this memoir. Interesting to later learn that Osama bin Laden, whose family owned a large construction company in Saudi Arabia, returned to Riyadh in 1989, after fighting the Russians in Afghanistan for two years. He left Riyadh again in April of 1991, just three months after we left to come home. His presence while we were there might have been a factor in the rising tensions in tribalism, the stresses of economic globalization, religious competition between Muslims and Christians, and cultural shifts between males and females we sensed during our stay. After 9/11, and before his death in May of 2011, Osama bin Laden was reportedly stripped of his Saudi Arabian citizenship.

When I officially retired from free-lance writing in 2011, I reread Jill Ker Conway's *From the Road to Coorain*. I also bought and read two other books she authored, *True North* written in 1994, and *When Memory Speaks*, written in 1998. Conway, along with many other gifted writers of memoir inspired me to complete the book you now hold in your hands. My desire was to write the story of our time in Saudi Arabia for our children and grandchildren, why we did what we did and how it affected me as a woman, and us as a couple. What Conway seemed to be saying in *From the Road to Coorain* about leaving Australia as a single young woman, first to England and then to the U.S., was how I perceived my experiences of leaving home.

The personal growth I experienced in Saudi Arabia isn't about who I had become, as much as a return to my authentic self. In writing this memoir, some 26 years later, I have come to realize my Saudi experience was the beginning of me rediscovering who God created me to be. Saudi Arabia became the link between my life before, and my life after, our mid-life adventure. Reflecting on all three periods in my life helped me understand how writing one's personal history can heal past hurts, deepen one's faith in God, open one's heart and mind to a greater awareness of the power of love, and change the direction and quality of one's life.

The writing took more effort, more energy and commitment than I first imagined. I don't tell you this, dear reader, to discourage you from writing your memoir. I hope you will if you have an interest and intention. As someone who has treasured the family histories compiled by my mother and my aunt, I wanted to do the same for our family of our time in Saudi Arabia. I also did it for us, especially for Andy.

Today, ISIS and other terrorist groups dominate international headlines and bring fear and instability to our world. Religious, political and cultural power struggles between ideologies, classes, even genders, increase our uncertainties of the future. Do we humans have the will to overcome our weaknesses of fear and jealousy, to learn compassion and forgiveness so we can create peace on Earth, goodwill to all?

My faith tells me the best place for any of us to begin is to forgive and love ourselves first so we can offer the same grace to others. One of my favorite quotes is this from Henry Wadsworth Longfellow: *"If we could read the secret history of our enemies, we should find in each man's life enough sorrow and suffering to disarm all hostility."*

We must begin the lifelong journey of knowing who we are under all the protective layers of pretending, defending, posturing and projecting, to reveal our authentic selves created by God as both human and divine.

Take the time to know what gives *your* life purpose and meaning. Do what you love and love what you do. Use your God-given gifts to help create a peaceful, just and sustainable world for all. It's the most important effort any of us can undertake during our lifetime. No effort with the intention to help others, regardless of how seemingly small and insignificant, is spent in vain.

To anyone reading this book to the end, I hope you are inspired to write at least a few stories from your own life after reading mine. Every life has stories worth sharing that help us connect with each other and ourselves in more compassionate ways. I thank you for your support of the three charities listed in the front of the book who will benefit from your generosity, and I wish you well in all your endeavors.

> I am content to follow to its Source
> Every event in action or in thought;
> Measure the lot; forgive myself the lot!
> When such as I cast out remorse
> So great a sweetness flows into the breast
> We must laugh and we must sing,
> We are blest by everything
> Everything we look upon is blest.
>
> —W.B. Yeats

References

www.eddieconner.com
www.grammarly.com
www.janlundy.com
www.markmatousek.com
www.personalhistorians.org
www.writersdigest.com

Coming Home to Ourselves: A Woman's Journey to Wholeness
by Jan Forrest-Lundy (out of print; PDF available on Jan's website above)

Inventing the Truth: The Art and Craft of Memoir
by William Zinsser

My Deepest Me
by Janice Lynne Lundy

The Enneagram ~ A Christian Perspective
by Richard Rohr and Andreas Ebert

The Gift of Stories: Practical and Spiritual Applications of Autobiography, Life Story and Personal Mythmaking
by Robert Atkinson

The Hero Within: Six Archetypes We Live By
by Carol S. Pearson

The Road from Coorain
by Jill Ker Conway

The Writer's Journey: Mythic Structure for the Writer
by Christopher Vogler

True North ~ A Memoir
by Jill Ker Conway

When Memory Speaks: Exploring the Art of Autobiography
by Jill Ker Conway

Writing to Heal the Soul: Transforming Grief and Loss Through Writing
by Susan Zimmermann

About the Author

After returning from Saudi Arabia, Pam and Andy made their home in Grand Rapids, Michigan, where Andy joined a rheumatology and internal medicine practice and Pam became a writer for the Spectrum Health and Helen DeVos Children's Hospital Foundation.

In 1999, Pam self-published *Women's Voices, Women's Visions: A Book of Days for the Third Millennium*, dedicated to her grandchildren and born and unborn children of the world; and in memory of her friend Diane Zarafonetis who, in 1988, started the first support group in West Michigan for women with breast cancer. In 2008, Pam served as executive producer of *The Gift of All—A Community of Givers*, a one-hour documentary about the history of giving and volunteerism in West Michigan. In 2011, Pam self-published *Through the Eyes of a Child: The Story of Helen DeVos Children's Hospital*. She is a member of the Junior Golden Rule Guild, the Butterworth Auxiliary, and the Association of Personal Historians.

Pam and Andy are members of Our Lady of Aglona Parish in Grand Rapids. Together, they have four married children, and six granddaughters and six grandsons, ages 4 to 18.

www.ingramcontent.com/pod-product-compliance
Lightning Source LLC
Chambersburg PA
CBHW070054080526
44586CB00013B/1054